Railroaded

The Homophobic Prosecution of Brandon Woodruff for His Parents' Murders

PHILLIP CRAWFORD JR.

Cover photo of Brandon Woodruff by Suzy Marx. Used with written permission of photographer.

ISBN-13: 978-1718940383
ISBN-10: 1718940386

CONTENTS

INTRODUCTION

In October 2005 Texas authorities charged Brandon Woodruff – then a 19-year-old freshman attending Abilene Christian University as an agribusiness major – with murdering his parents Norma and Dennis. It was a blood bath. The couple had been sitting together on a sofa before the television set on a Sunday evening in their double wide manufactured home in Royse City, a rural community in northeast Texas, and both were shot and stabbed multiple times in their faces. Brandon was arrested just a few days after the murders in a complete shock to the community. The teen boy was charismatic and well-liked. Friends universally described him as "fun-loving" and "a great guy," and by all accounts Brandon and his folks had a loving relationship. Even investigators conceded at the time of his arrest that they lacked the evidence to convict him. They had no eyewitnesses, no murder weapons, no bloody prints; there literally was nothing linking him to the horrific crime. However, the police charged Brandon Woodruff simply because he had been home from college that weekend, and was the last known person to see them alive before heading back and investigators didn't buy his alibi.

Unable to make the $1 million bail Brandon Woodruff sat in a jail cell at the Hunt County Detention Center in downtown Greenville for more than three years awaiting trial. The investigation was marred by repeated blunders which raised substantial questions whether exculpatory evidence was missed and incriminatory evidence was planted. For example, cell phone tower data would have pinpointed Brandon's whereabouts at the time of the murders but they were destroyed by the mobile carrier before their evidentiary value was recognized by law enforcement. A dagger which the state argued was a murder weapon was discovered by a family member on the eve of trial in a Woodruff barn, and yet earlier the investigators had searched it and found nothing. The blunders were so pervasive that the investigation is not entitled to any credibility; too many pieces of the puzzle simply are missing or suspicious in order to make a compelling case against Brandon Woodruff. The investigative mishaps may be attributable just to regrettable incompetence by law enforcement but that does not make the real consequences any less prejudicial for the hapless defendant.

However, the prosecution also involved outright misconduct. A freshly-minted junior prosecutor eavesdropped on jailhouse telephone conversations between Brandon Woodruff and his legal team. After the presiding judge ruled that the defendant's Sixth Amendment right to counsel was violated, the Hunt County District Attorney's Office recused itself. The Texas Attorney General took over the prosecution, and a top prosecutor from that office then launched a smear campaign against Brandon Woodruff before the public from which the jury would be selected and in front of the judge to whom the case was assigned. For example, the assistant attorney general advised the public that Brandon Woodruff had performed in gay porn. True, but irrelevant and inflammatory. The prosecutor then further told the presiding judge that those films may involve underage boys. False, and perhaps a fatal blow to Brandon's standing before the judge who ruled repeatedly against the young defendant on key issues. The films in which Brandon Woodruff appeared were produced by a legitimate studio which complied with federal record-keeping requirements to ensure all performers were in fact adults. Of course, the state prosecutor could have verified all this before dropping an inflammatory bomb against Brandon Woodruff but sadly no opportunity was lost to smear him.

In March 2009 when the case finally was presented to a jury in the heart of the Bible belt, the prosecution essentially posited during the 12-day trial that Brandon Woodruff was living a double life who killed when his worlds supposedly collided. Brandon was a horse wrangler and attending Abilene Christian University, and he also was a porn actor and dancing at Dallas gay clubs. Faced with flunking out and returning home to a hick town the state argued that Brandon killed his disappointed parents for their life insurance so he would be free to pursue his gay path with carefree abandon. There was no double life; just a boy coming out. The evidence introduced at trial on Brandon's homosexuality and his coming out was so prejudicial that the state prosecutors might as well have just called him The Talented Mr. Ripley, and the jury might as well have just convicted him for being gay. Indeed, eight jurors believed "that being homosexual or gay is morally wrong," and the jury convicted him after only five hours of deliberation. The state earlier had waived the death penalty out of consideration to the surviving family who already had lost Norma and Dennis, and Brandon Woodruff automatically was sentenced to a life term behind bars without any possibility of parole.

The incarceration rate for lesbian, gay and bisexual people is three times the general population according to the 2017 study *Incarceration Rates and Traits of Sexual Minorities in the United States* by The Williams Institute at UCLA School of Law. Dr. Ilan H. Meyer, one of the study's authors, said "we need to understand more about the pathways that lead to greater incarceration of LGB people and whether biases ingrained in the criminal justice system lead to sexual minorities being treated differently than heterosexuals." Unfortunately, "there are currently little study and available data on LGBT offenders at several points of the criminal process, including arrest and detention, charging, conviction, sentencing, and probation and parole" as noted by Professor Jordan Blair Woods from University of Arkansas in his 2017 article "LGBT Identity and Crime" for the *California Law Review*. However, some instances have been found where the "court system itself can be a hostile environment for homosexual criminal defendants" writes Michael Shortnacy in his 2001 article "Guilty and Gay" for the *American University Law Review*, and "prosecutors can shape legal outcomes with their biased behavior." The prosecution against Brandon Woodruff for his parents' murders is such a case.

The slipshod investigation, the insufficient evidence, the constitutional violations, the smear campaign and the homophobic narrative all contributed in the aggregate to deprive Brandon Woodruff of a fair trial. Heck, from start to finish, from arrest to conviction, Brandon Woodruff was railroaded. The lawmen believed they had their boy, and in seeking to convict him the end justified the means. And yet from day one Brandon Woodruff has maintained his innocence, and this is not just talk. A polygraph examination by a foremost expert concluded that Brandon Woodruff was truthful in his denials about killing his parents, and the result was confirmed by a subsequent test by another examiner. The statistical odds that both examinations would erroneously indicate a truthful response are less than two percent.

This book largely relies upon a voluminous record from the police investigation and judicial proceedings including video recordings from two dozen witness interviews, a 400-page investigative report, the transcripts from the pre-trial hearings and the 12-day trial, filings and exhibits thereto docketed with the court, and post-trial challenges including an appeal in the state system and writ of habeas corpus in federal court. Brandon Woodruff cooperated with this book, and he and some supporters including family and friends who long have stood by him provided additional insight and material.

During the investigation and subsequent trial some names were floated – specifically, Brandon's onetime friend Mike Etherington and his older sister Charla Woodruff – for police and jurors to consider. However, law enforcement previously had concluded that the evidence did not point to Mike or Charla, and at trial the jury convicted Brandon as his parents' killer. In reporting on these official proceedings this book makes no accusation or suggestion that either Mike Etherington or Charla Woodruff had any role in connection with the double murders. Although there is a compelling argument that Brandon Woodruff not only was deprived of a fair trial but actually may be innocent, the underlying investigation was so botched there is no basis to suspect anyone as the real killer. The so-called criminal justice system probably got the wrong guy, and yet it's otherwise still a complete mystery who the real killer may be. Indeed, even the name may be an unknown to law enforcement, and the individual has flown under its radar.

Perhaps the elusive Phantom Killer who once terrorized northeast Texas still is out there.

1 TEXAS BOYHOOD

Dennis Dale Woodruff and Norma Faye Johnston were high school sweethearts who met during the late 1970s at Arkansas High School in Texarkana where both played in the band. Their families had multi-generational roots in the area. Texarkana was established as a railway junction in southwest Arkansas which shares a border with its same-named sister town in northeast Texas, and the state line cuts right through the federal building. The Texarkana name is a mashup of Texas, Arkansas and Louisiana. Shreveport is just an hour's drive south.

Texarkana is in the Bible belt. The American Baptist Association is based in Texarkana on the Texas side, and during his preacher years Governor Mike Huckabee headed the Beech Street First Baptist Church on the Arkansas side. Of course, the devil rides the same streets as Jesus, and they're racing for the same souls. Evil long has given righteousness a run for the money in Texarkana. Decades ago in 1946 a serial killer in the Texarkana area was targeting romantic couples on both the Texas and Arkansas sides of the border, and in four separate shooting attacks killed five and wounded three. The victims were young adults in their cars on lovers' lanes, and a middle-aged married couple in their farmhouse. No one ever faced justice for these crimes, and the wicked soul who attacked the hapless sweethearts was dubbed the Phantom Killer.

If opposites attract, then Dennis and Norma were destined to be together. He was a strapping boy at six feet, and she was a petit girl barely over five feet and a hundred pounds. Dennis was born on September 26, 1962 as the oldest of four children by Clyde Dale Woodruff and Bonnie Sue Plunkett, and Norma was born on February 9, 1963 as the youngest of three by Ben Johnston and Opal Graf. The Woodruffs were town folk, and Dennis's father owned Dale's Discount Furniture and Appliance store and was active in the Chamber of Commerce and other community groups. The Johnstons were country folk, and Norma's father, a World War II veteran, worked at the Red River Army Depot, the largest employer in Texarkana, and he further raised a few cows and had horses. Dennis was strictly raised in the Walnut Church of Christ – located on the Texas side of Texarkana – which his "hardcore" family attended each Sunday without fail, and Norma belonged to the Hickory Street Baptist Church but family attendance was infrequent because her parents spent Sundays tending their vegetable garden. Dennis was affable and funny, and Norma was quiet and reserved. Dennis and Norma married on June 18, 1982 just a year after high school graduation. Norma's sister Linda Matthews said throughout their marriage the couple remained "best friends" who were "very loving and very close and, you know, would cuddle with each other, love on each other, just, you know, they were just really, really close."

The married couple attended Southern Arkansas

University in Magnolia; Dennis got a degree in electrical engineering, and Norma received one in accounting. After college they moved to Rowlett, Texas in Rockwall County on Lake Hubbard just 25 miles northeast of Dallas to pursue their careers and start a family. Dennis spent many years with DSC Communications/Alcatel, and then later at Flextronics, Inc. as a quality control auditor. Norma passed the CPA exam, and was a longstanding employee at Dal-Tile corporate headquarters. Their daughter Charla Annette was born on August 16, 1985, and son Brandon Dale the following year on September 6, 1986. Although only thirteen months apart in age the siblings were separated by two years in school. In speaking of his children Dennis Woodruff rarely referred to them by name but as "the girl" or "the boy."

Rockwall County had a split identity as country hick and suburban preppy as the community was folded into the Dallas/Fort Worth metroplex. The Woodruff family was solidly middle class, and in the mid-1990s when Brandon and Charla still were in grammar school they settled into a modest 3-bedroom 2-bath one-story ranch-style brick home at 608 Laurence Drive. The house was built in 1969, and also had a white metal out building – they called it a barn – and two-acre back pasture. Just a few minutes away from the Woodruff residence was the beautiful top-ranked 18-hole Buffalo Creek Golf Club which opened in 1992, and surrounded by upscale homes. Rockwall County is among the wealthiest counties in Texas. The Woodruff couple moved to the Dallas area for economic opportunity but they intended to retire someday to their native Texarkana where they had purchased 20 acres.

The sibling rivalry between Charla and Brandon developed early, and only would exacerbate in later years. They both were adorable looking but the blond-haired blue-eyed Brandon had an infectious charisma that eclipsed his older sister. Brandon fondly was described by his Aunt Linda as "all boy" and a "mischievous little thing." When the young children were told to stay in the house after school while the parents still were at work Charla would dutifully – even if resentfully – comply but Brandon would disobey and hit the neighborhood to play. Given his impish personality Brandon's parents took him to an open audition for the title role in the Warner Bros. film *Dennis the Menace* – he didn't get the part – which was released in 1993.

When off work Norma was a jeans-and-t-shirt woman true to her country roots who liked getting her hands dirty hauling hay, building fences, raising animals and riding horses including her Missouri Fox Trotter named Honey. She was the baby of the family – brother Bob was older by eleven years and sister Linda by thirteen years – and adored by the family. Linda described Norma as "kind of everybody's favorite and could have been really spoiled but she wasn't," and was known as "just very generous and loving and caring and kind of always there for you when you needed her." Norma opened her big heart to Rockwall County. She was quite active with Equest which uses horseback riding as a therapeutic tool for disabled children, participated in the Komen Race for the Cure to raise money for breast cancer research, and at Christmas organized a toy and food collection among her co-workers at Dal-Tile for needy families.

Dennis had no interest in a ranching lifestyle, and spent most of his free time inside the home doing the cooking and cleaning. A family acquaintance said he was not "a manly man." Instead of an interest in sports Dennis Woodruff was a big fan of Dolly Parton, Cher, Tina Turner and Bette Midler. Indeed, Dennis was a tad obsessive about Dolly, and had collected her memorabilia since he was a fourteen-year-old boy all of which was displayed in its own room of the house aptly known as the Dolly Room. Dennis would rock out to Tina Turner's "Proud Mary" blaring from the stereo system without a care who may be watching. The family attended Dolly concerts and took trips to Dollywood. Charla once quipped that instead of a mom and dad she had two mommies: Dolly and Norma.

Norma Woodruff shared her passion for raising animals with Brandon and Charla. The two children both participated in 4-H and Future Farmers of America but it was Brandon who was blessed with Doctor Dolittle's gift of talking to the animals. Brandon just loved all creatures. He once raised a nest of buzzard chicks and an armadillo, and through the 4-H program with which his mother actively was involved Brandon raised just about everything from rabbits and lambs to hogs and cows. He won multiple Grand Champion awards at the Texas State Fair, and by high school had earned such respect for his work that others hired him to walk their stock in the ring.

Todd Williams was the Rockwall County extension agent, and ran the 4-H program including the so-called "ag barn" at which the kids boarded their livestock. Todd and his wife Tracy lived in a single-wide trailer on the same property as the ag barn. The Williams couple was long-time personal friends of the Woodruff family, and had known Brandon since he was in the fifth grade. Todd described Brandon as "a good kid, enthusiastic" who "wanted people to like him, and attracted attention just because people liked him." From all observations Brandon "loved his parents" said Todd, and "at various points he would hug his mom and he would joke with his dad." Todd's wife Tracy said Brandon "has a gift and an aptitude for working with animals," and "I think he could make a very lucrative career in showing animals."

Horses were Brandon's favorite particularly a black-and-white Andalusian named Czar which he trained to lay down, bow, rear and chase after him. When Norma was pregnant with Brandon she suffered a nasty fall from a horse, and she often joked Brandon got the "horse bug" as a result of that while still in the womb. With his affinity for showmanship Brandon ultimately took up trick riding, and then in 2003 while performing at an exhibition had his own fall in which he broke both ankles and was confined to a wheelchair. Dennis Woodruff took time off from work, and was nursemaid to the boy. "For six months I couldn't walk," Brandon said "but when I got back on, I could get back on bareback without a halter and lead her up and let's go run." Many remarked that the high school boy had "a natural talent" with horses, and he should consider a career as a professional wrangler. Laurie Wilder, the owner and operator of the EZL Equine Boarding facility, would hire Brandon when she was out of town to "care for the horses in my boarding facility," and she "was very impressed by his maturity and professionalism and always felt secure that my home and animals were being dutifully cared for."

Growing up Brandon was all cowboy. He dressed in Wrangler blue jeans, pearl snap shirts and Lucchese western boots, and his leather belts sported engraved buckles won for showing livestock at state fairs. His conversation was sprinkled with Texas idioms like "y'all" and "guaran-damn-tee." Often he was shirtless and barefoot whether just driving around town, mudding along trails in four-wheelers or working in the barn, and photos from high school show him riding Czar bareback in a half-dressed state. "That was Brandon," said Tamara Keel who boarded the Woodruff horses and described herself as "his second mother," and "it didn't matter what type of weather he'd be with always no shirt, no shoes." She said:

> I was always constantly telling him to put his shirt on. He was always getting out of his truck or his mother's car that he would drive sometimes with no shoes and no shirt at the barn. And I would tell him, you have to get dressed before he could go mess with his horses.

In 2003 Brandon began working at Chisholm Feed Store after school and on Saturdays, and lifting the heavy bags put a little definition on his lanky 6-foot tall frame. The feed store was owned by husband-and-wife Randy and Ede Bullock, and they had known Brandon and his family as customers for years before the teen started working for them. Ede Bullock described Brandon as "a great kid" who worked hard and "never had his hand in the till."

Throughout most of high school Brandon ran with the "shit kickers": boys like himself involved with showing livestock and dressing cowboy. In addition to Brandon the pack comprised Michael "Mike" Etherington, Joseph "Joe" Hagaman and Dustin "Dusty" Perry. The four boys ate lunch together at a round table in the school cafeteria, and Mike said "all of us were real close like brothers" and "had each other's back."

Brandon and Mike had known each other since grade school, and in the 4-H shows a long-existing competitive rivalry existed between them. Mike came from a broken home. His mother worked for the IRS, and his father built drag racers. They divorced when Mike and his brother Matt were just two- and four-years-old, respectively. Mike claimed his older brother used him as a "punching bag" until one day in high school Mike – he'd grown into a rugged lad at 6' 1" and 165 pounds – fought back and decked Matt across the jaw. By some accounts Brandon's parents did not much approve of Mike Etherington, and Todd Williams characterized him as "bad news." Brandon claimed that Mike and Joe once stole from a horse expo:

> You know the Paint World Show? He [Mike] was involved in like a major – like it made, like, the papers about there being a lot of thefts and stuff in that room. Well, that's because him and Joseph Hagaman walked out with four pairs of ostrich-skin boots and necklaces, and you wouldn't – you wouldn't believe some of the stuff that they got.

Joe Hagaman, a husky boy at 5'9" and 210 pounds, was closer to Mike than Brandon, and through 4-H raised and showed cows at the state fair. The theft allegations have not been corroborated, and Mike and Joe presumably deny them.

Brandon became particularly close with Dustin Perry during high school. Dustin's nickname to most people was "Dusty" but Brandon and the other shit kickers called him by his last name "Perry." Dusty was an FFA member who raised horses and worked for a veterinarian hospital. He expressed admiration for Brandon's "good eye" in selecting livestock, and his ability to raise them and re-sell the prize winners for a tidy profit.

Brandon Woodruff was quite popular in high school, and Mike Etherington said he was an "outgoing kid" always at the "center of attention." For example, Brandon donned his sister Charla's cheerleading outfit for high school pep rallies, wore a wig at the rodeo, and go-go danced shirtless on a car roof in the parking lot. At the local IHOP where the teen kids would loiter until the midnight hour Brandon strolled through the restaurant randomly talking to strangers, and on New Year's Eve in 2005 walked into the chain diner wearing nothing but a Mexican poncho, a cowboy hat and his boots. Sometimes his attention-grabbing antics bordered on obnoxious – like climbing on the back of a big girl and riding her like a bull – but when challenged the fun-loving Brandon would tone it down rather than risk a fight. On the whole his good-natured play was appreciated, and in senior year his classmates voted him as having the most school spirit.

The Woodruff household was not without some dysfunction as with any family, and both parents had their own personal struggles as does everyone. Norma Woodruff was described as always looking stressed out. She worked hard at Dal-Tile, often putting in late hours, and actively was involved – perhaps too much so – in her children's activities. Norma was a bit of a hoarder, and she stacked newspapers everywhere. Although many friends and family characterized Dennis Woodruff as gentle and funny some claimed he also had an angry and dark side. The once-lean Dennis had ballooned in weight, and at one point underwent a gastric bypass to restrict food consumption. At the time of his death Dennis weighed 375 pounds which in clinical terms is morbidly obese. Dennis's sister Kathy Lach said the only time she ever had seen her brother cry was when their father Clyde died in 2004, and he was inconsolable and "cried hard." Both parents were night owls who stayed up until two or three in the morning at their computers.

Charla said that she "really did not get along at home" with her parents, and "had a lot of problems growing up with them, a lot." According to Charla "my dad had a huge temper," and she suffered "borderline abusive" spankings and whippings into her early teens from him that left hand imprints and belt marks on her ass. However, perhaps Charla's abuse claims should be viewed with healthy skepticism. For example, Brandon said that although he and his sister were spanked, Charla has greatly over-dramatized the discipline. Next-door neighbor Randall "Randy" Lunz, a procurement manager in the real estate division at a multi-finance company, had known the Woodruffs for nearly a decade, and he said "Dennis had a soft heart" and "I never saw him lay a hand on those kids." Lunz characterized the Woodruff couple as "very good parents": "They were very active with their children. Their children came first. Seemed like a pretty close family." Linda Matthews, Norma's sister, denied hearing any allegations that Dennis ever abused Charla.

Regardless of whether Dennis Woodruff was ever "borderline abusive" to Charla, her rage against him was real. The anger was more than just teenage rebellion, and sometimes erupted into violent attacks. Dennis Woodruff had to call the police to the family home when Charla, fifteen at the time, physically attacked him. On another occasion as Dennis was driving the car Charla in the back seat attempted to kick out a side window. The girl spat less venom against her mother but hardly was a fan. When asked if Dennis ever hit Norma, Charla said "no," and then immediately sounded almost disappointed: "and that's what I never understood – my mom could do no wrong."

In high school Charla became convinced that her parents were cheating on each other, and confronted them with her suspicions. She pointed out that her mother often worked late, and her father regularly spoke about a girl at the office. The Woodruff couple dismissed Charla's concerns about their marital fidelity, and were at their wit's end in trying to reason with her. The reality is that Norma and Dennis Woodruff were consumed by going to work and raising kids. Norma and Dennis rarely socialized with their own peer group, and most of their activities outside of work were with their kids. As Joe Hagaman said about the Woodruff parents: "they did everything that their kids did." However, nothing ever was enough for the high-maintenance Charla, and throughout high school she griped about one thing after another with the family.

Charla also admitted to bullying her brother during their childhood through assaults and harangues. Charla resentfully spoke about Brandon as the cute one whom she believed was the family favorite. Over the years the fighting between the two went well beyond sibling rivalry, and their relationship became so ugly that grandparents only would have one child over at a time in order to maintain peace. Charla's fixation on Brandon was known in the community and extended family. For example, Maryann Scudder, a Woodruff neighbor whose children also were active in Rockwall 4-H, said "there have always been some tension between Brandon and Charla through the years, but I attributed it to sibling rivalry, and also to the fact that Charla has had emotional issues during the time I knew her."

The girl's jealousy over her brother and antipathy against her parents were inexplicable, and by all accounts Norma and Dennis Woodruff showered Charla with love and support even if she was unable to appreciate it. They gave Charla her own horse, and Norma coached her softball team. In high school Charla was a member of the state-renowned Rockwall Stingerette drill team, and her parents paid for all her expenses associated with its extensive travel for special events including ocean cruises. Just days after her parents' murders Charla disturbingly giggled about "playing them" to get whatever she wanted. If Charla did not get what she wanted then like King Baby would have a hissy fit which included holding her breath until she passed out; however, this behavior immediately stopped once her parents said she would not be able to obtain a driver's license if these spells persisted.

Moreover, Charla Woodruff was a pretty girl and popular in high school. Although only 5'5" the long-haired blond had a voluptuous build which did not go unnoticed among the boys, and one of Brandon's friends "talked about how his sister looked good." Many of Charla's friends were older siblings of Brandon's friends. For example, for a time in high school her best friend was Mike Etherington's older brother Matt, and Charla was sufficiently friendly with the Etherington family that she called their mother – also named Norma – Mama E. Dustin Perry said that Charla once dated his older brother, too.

Charla's behavioral problems were well-known among the Woodruff family and friends. For example, one professional colleague of Dennis Woodruff said "all of Dennis's work friends knew that Charla was the problem child." During high school she even attempted suicide on multiple occasions including once with her father's loaded semi-automatic handgun. As Charla stated, "I tried to kill myself when I was 14 with a gun but I messed up. I messed up the gun." It's unclear why the firearm failed to fire although perhaps its safety was on or it did not feed properly. Throughout this period Charla's parents and little brother provided consistent support for the troubled girl.

After graduating in May 2003 Charla went to community college that summer, and then in the fall matriculated at her parents' alma mater Southern Arkansas University in Magnolia. Dennis and Norma visited her for every home football game played by the Muleriders, and they called her every night. One of Dennis's close friends and co-workers from DSC/Alcatel said "it shocked me when he said he called her every night when she went off to college" but Dennis explained "it was out of concern for her" and "he said sometimes they didn't talk for long but they talked every day."

Ever since childhood Charla wanted to be a police officer, and was studying criminal justice at SAU. In December 2004 Charla gave a television interview to The SAU Report which was produced by the university's broadcast journalism department. Charla and a classmate had co-founded Supporting Women in Crisis which was a sexual assault crisis hotline and support group. The new group was not under university auspices but SWIC offered its services to SAU students as well as the Magnolia community. Charla explained to the student interviewer that she had a personal motivation for co-founding the organization: "I was raped when I was six years old. Growing up confused whether sex was bad, sex was good, what this was about. I was mentally confused. I was very confused."

Perhaps Charla's publicly-admitted childhood rape contributed to her desire to enter law enforcement. In the interview Charla explained why she chose to major in criminal justice:

> Ever since I was young I imagined being a cop, and I don't know if it was a fascination with guns or if it was the authority or the power. But I really want to

have the chance to give back to the community and offer a community protection and security where they live.

Of course, her suicide attempt with a firearm in high school and continued apparent "fascination with guns" in college could pose a stumbling block for her career goal.

Dennis and Norma were not "holy rollers." The children went to public school and participated in secular activities. Dennis enjoyed his food, and even some vices like chewing tobacco and a little porn. The old man had a porn collection of 40 or 50 VHS tapes and several dozen magazines which Brandon said he and Charla had discovered in their early teens:

> We'd let our friends look at them, borrow them, and it was all at about 13, 14 years old until my dad found out we'd found them. Yeah, we both got grounded for that one! But then, later on my dad bought the Paris Hilton porn DVD and made a point to actually show me where he had it. He didn't know I had already found it and watched it. So porn was just kinda "around." Never really a big deal.

Norma and Dennis were not big drinkers but they also were not teetotalers. The Woodruffs occasionally attended the Church of Christ in Rockwall, and when visiting extended family in Texarkana would go to the Walnut Street Church where Brandon participated in the youth group. Both Brandon and Charla were baptized in their early teens.

In the fifth grade Brandon was introduced to the Mount Fort Christian Camp in Beavers Bend State Park in southeastern Oklahoma, and each summer he attended for a week right through high school graduation. Brandon described the camp as "a scenic place" with "no phones, no cars" where he has "nothing but good and fun memories of," and "we were a real close group of kids at camp and most all of us would return year after year." At summer camp after his high school freshman year Brandon met Eric Gentry from DeSoto, TX – the Gentry family originally was from San Antonio – whose father was a minister, and the two became steadfast friends. DeSoto was only a 30-minute ride southwest from Rockwall, and Brandon and Eric would visit each other throughout the year. Eric described Brandon as "the nicest guy you'll ever meet," and that was an assessment shared generally by fellow campers and camp staff. In the summer after his junior year, Brandon Woodruff was selected as Best Camper.

2 COMING OUT

In the second half of his high school senior year Brandon Woodruff began acknowledging that he may be gay. Even in 2005 it was a brave move for a teen boy to come out particularly in a conservative state like Texas. It was only two years earlier that the U.S. Supreme Court in the landmark case *Lawrence v. Texas* struck down the Lone Star State's sodomy statute pursuant to which gay men were imprisoned for sexual relations, and many religious conservatives citing the Biblical condemnation of homosexuality believe the high court overreached. The Human Rights Campaign, the nation's largest LGBT advocacy group, currently ranks Texas among the worst states on its equality index for sexual minorities given the lack of legal protections on basic matters. For example, Texas does not prohibit discrimination based on sexual orientation or gender identity in employment, housing and public accommodations, and it has no law to address bullying against queer kids in the schools or banning their psychological torture through conversion therapy. In 2017 the Texas legislature introduced more anti-LGBT bills than any other state in the country, and among those that passed was one which allows adoption agencies to refuse placing children with LGBT folk. It's still no little thing to be a gay boy in Texas.

Brandon discovered the gay clubs in Dallas, and acquired a new circle of friends in nearby Denton. The 18-year-old high school senior began dating guys, and considered 36-year-old Doug as his first boyfriend. Brandon may have loved his mother dearly but he was no mama's boy, and he'd routinely break curfew in order to explore his new world. Dennis Woodruff had given the boy a white 1995 Dodge truck that he recently inherited from his own father. Although the Dodge had 140,000 miles on it and a history of breaking down the truck was a ticket to freedom for Brandon out of provincial Heath into the big city. Norma told one friend she "was exacerbated" with Brandon, and told her sister Linda "I don't know what we're going to do with Brandon." Norma and Dennis always had been overly-protective of their children, and Brandon now was cutting the apron strings.

Growing up Brandon said that "my parents never brought up the gay issue," and "my dad was the one who had the 'sex talk' with me and he never fully talked on the gay issue then but just 'sex with a girl.'" While dating Doug in his senior year Brandon said that he told his father "on the possibility of me being gay," and his father had pressed the issue particularly because of the age difference between the two: "so my dad would call while I was with Doug and if I spent the night at his house because he was 36, my dad would want to know for sure."

The Woodruff couple may have had some concerns about Brandon being gay but they were not intolerant people. Dennis Woodruff had gay friends and co-workers he cared about, and on an occasion or two even had visited a gay bar. It's pretty hard to love musical icons such as Dolly, Cher, Bette and Tina without some openness to gay folk. However, Brandon said that Charla was particularly vicious with her suspicions that he was gay, and when the boy was in the eighth grade she allegedly "look[ed] at me directly in the eye," and spat out "I think you're a fucking faggot." Brandon further recounted that "my dad was furious at her use of words."

Brandon previously had dated a few girls, and he really dug Morgan Lee. She was a barrel racing cowgirl a year behind Brandon in school, and they met at a rodeo in 2002. Her mother Michelle – known in the community as Miss Lee – worked as a medical technician for a Dallas ophthalmologist, and her father Mike was a commercial real estate developer. They were an affluent family, and in 2005 were leasing a place at 1895 Creekside Drive in Rockwall, TX while building their dream home in nearby Poetry.

A few years after meeting the young teens started dating on-and-off, and in 2005 Brandon took Morgan to his senior prom. They double dated with Brandon's pal Dustin Perry and his girl, and Brandon drove them all in his mother's truck. Norma had a heavy duty ¾-ton capacity 2001 Chevy Silverado 1500 with a 4-door crew cab and leather interior, and it was a sweet upgrade from Brandon's old Dodge. Brandon coveted the Silverado but only was allowed to drive it with Norma's permission on special occasions like the prom or when he needed the more powerful vehicle to pull his stock or horse trailer when showing animals. However, he sometimes took it without asking, and once got pulled over for speeding in it. Boosting the family car for a joyride is an all-American boyhood experience, and is a staple in coming-of-age movies such as *Risky Business* where Tom Cruise as Joel Goodsen takes out his old man's Porsche or *Ferris Bueller's Day Off* where Matthew Broderick as the title character borrows a red Ferrari. Boys will be boys, and sometimes they can be a bit naughty.

Once he started dating boys Brandon changed his style. He stopped dressing cowboy and became more trendy wearing designer clothes such as Armani and Abercrombie & Fitch. He started tanning, bleaching his hair, and got his ears and nipples pierced. In short, he started flaming, and it was becoming increasingly obvious to everyone that Brandon was gay even if he did bother to expressly say so. Brandon stated that "other people would say they thought I was gay or come out and just say it like it was true," and "it never bothered me though because I was just me."

By spring 2005 the new changes in Brandon were not well accepted by his old friends who gossiped among each other whether he'd turned queer. Dustin Perry said he hoped Brandon was not gay but he "started acting kind of queer-like" which "got worse and worse." Joe Hagaman bemoaned that Brandon used to be a "normal person" but then "put out the gay vibe or whatever you want to call it when he started changing." Joe further said "I don't have a problem with gay people as long as they keep their distance, and you know, and don't try to move in on me, they're fine." Frankly, unless there was some chubby chaser at Rockwall High, it's hard to believe a gay boy was knocking on Joe's door for anything.

With derisive contempt Mike Etherington mocked Brandon's increasingly flamboyant style and feminine mannerisms. Mike said he doesn't have "any problem" with gay folk but was "uncomfortable" with them "flaunting it," and further was against gay marriage because he believed homosexuality was a "big sin":

> I'm totally against gay marriage. It's wrong, you know. It's totally wrong. It's a big sin and stuff. I don't have any problem with you being gay it's just if you're going to go around flaunting it in front of me or something like that it just makes me uncomfortable. I won't do anything.

Mike and his girlfriend attended the Pure Heart Fellowship in Rowlett and were active in its youth group. According to Mike an out kid in high school, Russell Gibson, was crushing on him, and the shit kicker set the record straight by showing his gay admirer pictures of his girlfriend:

> I talk to kids that are gay. I never had any problem with them. The rule goes for me "if you're gay and stay to yourself, we talk, that's fine." A kid all through my junior year sat behind me in physics class. We chit chat just fine but he started giving me food and candy every day and I started hearing from his friends, you know, his little girlfriends or whatever, that he had a little thing for me. I straight up told him "dude, just keep your distance on me." I made it real clear I had a girlfriend. I showed him pictures of my girlfriend, and told him about the date we had the previous evening. You know, it's nothing like "you're a faggot. I hate you, this and that."

At one point Brandon had hoped to bridge his new friends with the old crew, and on different occasions had introduced them but the meetings did not go well. Mike said he was creeped out by the Denton crowd. As Brandon recounted: "I was starting to venture out a little bit in Dallas. Just going in a different direction. Mike wasn't too happy about that, and so it kind of had a drift. Our relationship started to strain."

Brandon may not have expressly come out to his shit-kicking friends but he otherwise was putting it out there for acknowledgment, and they clearly were not digging his new self. Accordingly, Brandon attempted to move on, and at high school hung out less with the shit kickers and more with the Rockwall preps. Brandon said he was harassed with questions from his old friends: "Why are you wearing preppy clothes? Why are you going and hanging out with those people? What are you doing?" Brandon said "I felt like I didn't owe them any explanations because I was just kind of going into a different way. I was going into a different path in my life."

Todd Williams, the 4-H advisor who was a long-time friend of the Woodruff family, told Brandon to discontinue his relationship with Mike Etherington:

> That because of the falling out, he did need to leave Mike Etherington alone. They were people that he would have to go to school with at various points but he did not have to communicate with him, so those are the people that he needed to leave alone.

Brandon accepted Todd's advice, and told Mike he did not want to remain friends with the shit kickers because he now was hanging out with the Rockwall preps:

> But point come to chase. So when I told Mike that I didn't want to hang out with him anymore. Now I'm like, okay, you're not in my group, which I'm okay with. Like I had told him our family was going to cut all ties with him. You know what I'm saying? Like I can tell you – if I'm going to tell you that it's a done deal, it's a done deal. We're not going to talk about it

anymore. We're not going to bring it up anymore, you know.

However, some resentment continued simmering with the parting.

Things came to a dramatic head between Brandon and his old friends at the end of their senior year. In May 2005 someone egged Brandon's truck overnight as it sat on the driveway of the Heath home, and Brandon suspected Joe Hagaman was responsible. The next morning the aggrieved boy tracked Joe down in the high school parking lot, and threatened to bust his car windshield with a baseball bat he kept in the truck. The confrontation escalated into a dustup in which the two boys exchanged blows and wrestled on the ground until broken up by an intervening teacher. Apparently, the cops were called, both boys got cited and a judge put them on probation.

Other than that fight not a single person has recounted Brandon ever physically tangling with another. Brandon told Eric, his friend from church camp, about the fight, and Eric characterized it as just a one-off event for the otherwise easy-go-lucky teen:

> Brandon was kind of a wiener. He didn't have an attitude at all. Not a temper at all. If me and Brandon ever got into an argument Brandon would just start laughing and then I would start laughing. He was never violent or mad and never showed any kind of aggression. I never saw Brandon fighting or being violent at all. Plus he was scrawny. I don't think he could have fought somebody if he wanted to.

Indeed, multiple people described Brandon as a "wiener" who avoided conflict.

Although Brandon had said goodbye to his old shit

kicker pals and found a new circle of gay friends, he still maintained a close relationship with Morgan Lee and Eric Gentry. Eric also noted that Brandon had started appearing more "feminine" in his "flaming shirts" and styled hair, and said that Brandon complained about Mike Etherington and Joe Hagaman "teaming up" against him. Morgan suspected that Brandon was gay, too, and she liked his makeover. Morgan said Brandon used to wear "Wranglers and boots and stuff like that, not really caring too much, just, you know, comfortable," and then he became "a little more stylish, up with it, and dressing up a little more, taking care of himself, looking good." In the summer of 2005 after high school graduation Eric would drive up from DeSoto to visit Brandon, and they would hang out with Morgan riding horses, mudding along trails in ATVs and jumping on the trampoline.

Meanwhile, Mike Etherington had become oddly fixated on Brandon Woodruff and his sexual orientation. It was as if Mike were a jilted lover, and unable to accept that Brandon had moved on with his life. Mike cyberstalked Brandon and poured over his MySpace page, and determined that his former boy had a lot of gay friends. Mike asked around town for gossip on Brandon. Russell Gibson now was working at the local Walmart, and he supposedly told Mike that he spotted Brandon in a shirtless contest at a gay bar, and Brandon then ended up in another guy's lap. A girl who went to that same bar with a bachelorette party on another occasion advised Mike she saw Brandon go-go dancing and kissing guys. Brandon no longer was dating Morgan – although the pair remained dear friends – but Mike warned Morgan and her parents that Brandon was gay. "Can you believe that your boyfriend or ex-boyfriend whatever is gay and stuff," Mike told Morgan. Her parents told Mike they were not surprised, and according to him Miss Lee said "Morgan, we need to get you tested for sexually transmitted diseases," and Mike Lee told her "I never liked that kid" and "you just need to stay away from that kid."

Brandon was reaching a boiling point with his onetime friends, and in late July or early August posted the following message on his MySpace page to make it clear that he was over them: "I would never regret anything in life . . . except a girl named Morgan Lee talking to nothing but trash like Dustin Perry (goofy ass nerd), Joseph Hagaman (who Jenny Craig couldn't help), Jerry Hemahosa (damn fat ass Mexican), and, yes, Mike Etherington (two-faced bitch)."

In saying good riddance to his old friends there was no looking back for Brandon. He had discovered an exciting new world in the Dallas gay scene, and in the summer of 2005 been accepted into a popular circle of cute boys many of whom came from affluent families. It was not a hard partying crowd – Brandon did not smoke, never tried drugs and rarely drank more than a beer – but they did have lots of good old-fashioned fun including weekend pool parties, amusement park trips and club hopping adventures. And since they were gay twinks there was much silliness and some cattiness. Brandon said "the movie *Mean Girls* had come out and some would call people in the group 'the plastics' but it was all in due fun."

The "plastics" revolved around Alexander Rulli who lived in Plano. Alex was a 20-year-old cater waiter and attending Collin County Community College. His dad was a successful businessman who often was out of town, and Brandon said "he'd have pretty big parties every weekend almost and I'd always be invited so I'd go, chill, swim, and just hang out," and "usually a lot of us like 15-20 would hang out at his house or his dad's house before we went to the clubs." As Alex said:

> Depending on what was going on, Saturday nights, we had a really close group of friends. We'd either hang out at someone's house, parties and stuff, and then Sunday nights, we'd — there's a club we always went to, it was 18 and up, and a lot of us could go out and there was usually a big crowd out there.

Alex said he and Brandon hung out "quite frequently," and they even "dated for a period of time." Alex's best friend was James Britt, and he characterized Brandon as "pretty personable":

> For a while he was new to the group so he was quiet, and just kind of stayed in the background. Never had any fights with anyone. He was a really nice person who got along with pretty much everyone. Never had a temper, not at all.

James further said Brandon "always seemed like he had money" and "was real generous," and "when we go out and stuff like that he'd pay for Alex or he'd pay for the group and never expected anything back."

Their favorite club was Station 4 or S4 which on Wednesday and Sunday nights was 18 and up. The club was located at 3911 Cedar Springs Road in the Oak Lawn neighborhood of downtown Dallas. Oak Lawn is a gayborhood, and Cedar Springs is "the Strip." The Strip is home to many gay bars, shops and restaurants, and the pride parade proceeds down it each year. Oak Lawn is home for many affluent gays who enjoy the green spaces, the upscale amenities and rich counter-culture history. In some ways, Oak Lawn is to Dallas what Greenwich Village is to New

York City or Old Town is to Chicago. Station 4 has long been the premier club in the gayborhood, and was a cavernous space with a dance floor, multiple rooms and an outdoor patio where folks could sit and talk away from the noise. On Sunday nights the cover charge for the under-21 kids was $10 but the drinking-age folk got in for free. At the club Brandon said "I really enjoyed dancing and the music," and "now, I could dance, quite well too and would dance down to my boxer briefs at times." On Wednesday nights Station 4 had a hip-hop style dance contest or "dance off" in which Brandon liked to participate, and he said "I have like a lot of dancing in me."

The exhibitionist teen on the dance floor caught the eye of a rep from Helix Studios which was a San Diego-based porn outfit known for its pretty boys or "twink" models in their late teens and early twenties with slender builds and hairless torsos. The Helix rep explained that the porn business "gets a bad reputation" but it "can be clean," and Brandon could set his "own rules." Brandon was flattered by the attention, and thought the Helix rep "was a pretty good guy." Accordingly, as a self-described "spontaneous guy who lived for the moment," Brandon went for it. He said "I wrote my own terms out stating that I'd never be a 'bottom' nor would anything ever go near my butt because I had no interests ever going in that direction ever while I was out there and so I played a role in which all my terms were met." Brandon said he "had no plans to ever make it a career or anything" but simply accepted it as an "adventure" which "was really fun to me at that time as crazy as it sounds." He described the filming as "not gross but really professional," and "you had set up teams, light guys, and most of the guys that played my role had girlfriends as well."

Studio head Keith Miller said Brandon "filmed a total of 5 scenes over two periods of time for Helix Studios" under the stage name Bradley Rivers. The first period was in July 2005 in Dallas, Texas, and involved filming three scenes over three days. Brandon filmed a scene on July 22 with Ricky Spears for *Tightend Twinks*, on July 23 with Ethan Stevens for *Boys N Toys* and then on July 24 in a three-way with Ricky and Ethan for *Pool Party Punks*. Brandon was paid $1,000 for his work in the three movies. The second period was in August 2005 in Fort Lauderdale, Florida, and involved two scenes over two days for *Pool Party Punks*. Brandon filmed a scene on August 19 with Jonathan Blaine and on August 20 in a three-way with Mason and Trevor. He also got a gig to film some action in New York which later was cancelled but Brandon still got paid $3,000.

Gay boys often dip their toes into porn work, go-go dancing or escorting even if only for a brief period as they explore their sexuality in the coming out process, and it's more common than many folks realize. After years of self-loathing repression in response to the drumbeat from family, church and society that homosexuality is wrong, there is something quite liberating about affirming one's desirability through adult entertainment and the sex trade before an appreciative audience. And heck, the boy had some wild oats to sow. Brandon told friends that he was modeling – albeit not in porn flicks which most performers are relatively discrete about, hence the use of stage names – and he even uploaded a few PG-13 images from his porn shoots to his MySpace page. In one still from *Pool Party Punks* the boy is standing poolside with thumbs tucked at the sides under his Speedo preparing to slip it off.

3 COLLEGE DAYS

Brandon Woodruff was not a studious boy in high school, and had a mediocre record. In fact, he even failed an economics class in his last semester at Rockwall High, and did not have the credits to graduate with his class in May 2005. In order to earn his diploma the boy had to attend summer school. It's not that Brandon wasn't bright (although he could be a tad dizzy) or lacked self-discipline (although he could be a bit impulsive); rather, he just applied himself to other pursuits. He was a conscientious and hard worker at the Chisholm Feed Store, and he was diligent in the daily care for his animals. Brandon simply would rather be outdoors doing something physical or with other people having fun rather than cooped up indoors with his nose in a book. The academic life simply was not for Brandon, and a round peg cannot be forced into a square hole.

And yet in his senior year Brandon applied to Abilene Christian University in West Texas which is governed by a Board of Trustees affiliated with the Church of Christ. Brandon said his application was "on a whim" upon the prompting of Eric Gentry from church camp. Eric's sister attended ACU, and Eric was applying there with the goal of becoming a preacher like his father. Eric said if Brandon also attended the two could be roommates, and without any thought Brandon just said "yeah." ACU requires a preacher recommendation for each applicant, and Eric's father wrote the one for Brandon. Brandon was accepted only on a conditional basis which placed him on scholastic probation at the outset due to his poor high school grades. The February 23, 2005 acceptance letter from ACU states:

> A review of your application file has been completed and we are pleased to offer you a conditional acceptance to ACU for the fall of 2005 semester. Because of your class rank in high school, we are admitting you on scholastic probation, which means you have one semester to make a 2.0 or higher overall grade point average in your classes. If you do not achieve this, you will be placed on academic suspension and not allowed to continue for the next semester.

Freshman orientation – called "welcome week" or "passport week" – at Abilene Christian University began on August 15, 2005, and Brandon settled into his dorm room with Eric Gentry in Mabee Hall which was an all-male freshman residence. ACU did not have co-ed dorms. Brandon the horse wrangler was enrolled as an ag business major, and Eric the preacher's son was enrolled as a Bible studies major. Brandon transformed their room into a man cave. He bought a flat screen TV and sound system for the dorm room, and decorated it with a Medieval-style dagger and a floor lamp made from an old rifle. And the place would not be Brandon's without a critter, and so he acquired a boa which he fed with live rats. The pet was against ACU rules and Eric did not like the stink but as a good friend Eric never said anything about it. Brandon did not have his own computer, and Eric let Brandon borrow his.

A social butterfly like Brandon had no problem making new friends. The incoming class was introduced to each other during welcome week through structured activities including a Twister marathon where multiple plastic game mats were laid out on the gymnasium floor. The kids also produced the Freshman Follies which is a revue-style performance with comedy skits and musical numbers, and in auditioning for it Brandon beat out many declared theater majors to land the lead Masters of Ceremonies role. Brandon's parents visited ACU the first weekend in October to see his performance in the Freshman Follies. "I was really proud of myself for that" Brandon said, and he considered changing his major from ag business to theater "but my dad did tell me that he would like – wanted me to think about it." Brandon said "my dad always told me, like, to make logical decisions and really, you know, like, decisions that will make me the future."

Eric already was friendly with many of the incoming freshman due to church ties, and they warmly embraced Brandon. The core group included Tim Applewhite, a 6'2" 300-pound big boy, and Adrienne Linge, a 5'2" 125-pound sweet girl. Tim and Adrienne had been dating since they met in their sophomore year of high school at a church event in San Antonio, and Eric had known Tim since grade school in San Antonio before the Gentry family moved to DeSoto. Tim was studying accounting and finance, and Adrienne wanted to become an elementary school teacher. Another girl in the circle was Lindsey Ferguson. She and Eric met for the first time at ACU but they had many friends in common due to church activities over the years, and they quickly became best friends. Lindsey was a blond-haired blue-eyed petite creature – she was just 5'3" and 115 pounds – enrolled as interior design major, and her dad was a Dallas cop. Rounding out the group was Tom Crews on the college baseball team whom Eric also had known from his boyhood years in San Antonio. The college kids had a lot of good-natured fun in Abilene including trips to the zoo, shopping at the mall and renting boats on the lake.

Everyone from the group just loved Brandon. Lindsey said "a lot of people liked him" because he was "a very friendly guy, very fun-loving":

> Loved to entertain people, was everybody's friend, just made people laugh all the time, just crazy, loved to go shopping, loved to mess with his hair, just a fun guy. He was always joking and kidding around. Friends with everybody.

Similarly, Adrienne characterized Brandon as "always a lot of fun and very entertaining":

> I thought he was a great guy. I have so many fond memories of him. He was just a real fun, fun kid. He was always happy. I can't remember a time of him being aggressive or angry. That's why I like being around him, you know. He's a different kind of kid. Always has been. Love him. Always have, always will.

In regard to his style, Adrienne said "he liked to stand out," and he "frequently liked to change his hair color and do fun things with his hair" and "he liked to wear neat outfits, you know."

Brandon was generous with his classmates, and quick to pick up a tab or buy a gift for them. Adrienne said

Brandon "was really generous with his money," and "he would throw money around a lot." Brandon picked up a $114 pair of jeans for one of Lindsey's girlfriends and a nice necklace for another, and Lindsey said: "He always had a lot of cash. He was throwing money around like crazy. Brandon was just generous like that. He loved to make people happy. He did have a lot of cash all the time."

For Tim Applewhite's birthday on October 6 the kids prepared him a celebration dinner, and Brandon paid half the grocery bill. Tim said Brandon "would always offer to purchase things for people or didn't mind spending money on every other person." After the birthday dinner they all went to the Oplin Dancehall. The Oplin was an old gymnasium which decades ago was turned into a dance floor, and ACU students were allowed to patronize the establishment because it was alcohol-free, had clean management and attracted a reputable crowd. The off-campus rules by which students must comply are so strict that even attending a club which serves alcohol is grounds for probation. Brandon kicked up a storm at the Oplin, and Lindsey said "Brandon doesn't country dance at all, and I watched him dancing all over girls, not country dancing, just like dirty dancing."

ACU was an unfortunate choice for Brandon given its restrictions on student conduct. Among its many rules students are required to attend daily chapel services between 11:00 and 11:30 a.m., not have pre-marital sex and respect an 11:00 p.m. curfew. Homosexuality is incompatible with the ACU mission. After ACU refused even to allow its students to form a Gay-Straight Alliance, President Phil Schubert explained in an April 25, 2011 article from *The Christian Chronicle*, an international newspaper for the Churches of

Christ, that the university's position for "faculty, staff and students" is clear in that "sex is reserved for the marriage bond between one man and one woman," and "we do not believe homosexual behavior is condoned in the Bible." ACU and Brandon were not a good match. However, when Brandon applied in fall 2004, he had not yet taken his first steps in dealing with his gay identity, and he said ACU's position on the subject was not a factor he ever considered: "really, homosexuality was not even really discussed at church camp nor church. At least not when I went." What a difference a year can make in a young gay boy's life as he finds himself.

Although not expressly out to his ACU classmates there certainly was some gossip about Brandon. His roommate Eric Gentry had known Brandon for years, and he remarked on how Brandon now appeared more "feminine" due to the "flaming shirts" which replaced the cowboy garb. Lindsey Ferguson said that "when I first met Brandon I was convinced he was gay. Convinced, like completely. Everybody that's met Brandon is convinced that he's gay at first." Adrienne Linge said Brandon "dressed like a homosexual" and "danced like a girl":

> He dressed like a homosexual. You know, not very many boys wear tight jeans and tight shirts and, you know, do their hair all the time. He did appear that way. We've heard from other places that he is gay, and I wouldn't have a hard time believing it, you know. I would have questions because when we did go dancing one time I just thought he danced like a girl, and I was like that was so strange to me. I was like you know most boys don't get out there in front of everybody and start dancing. Boys are kind of

cautious about going out and what shall I wiggle. I had a hard time on deciding on his sexuality because he told us he wasn't but sometimes it was questionable.

Nevertheless, none of that diminished a genuine affection for Brandon Woodruff from his ACU friends. They also were aware of his modeling. Sure, they did not know that some of it involved porn, but Brandon also was doing conventional work for a high-end Dallas stylist, and he showed them his book. As Adrienne Linge said: "He had shown us his portfolio. We really thought he was a model and everything. The portfolio was really nice. He had great pictures in there. It was absolutely believable." Accordingly, they all were aware that Brandon had activities outside of ACU. Indeed, during the school's welcome week Eric even drove Brandon to the local airport to catch a flight for a model shoot in Fort Lauderdale on August 19 and 20. Eric just did not know the shoot was filming for *Pool Party Punks*.

The academic semester began on August 22, and from the get-go Brandon was breaking curfew, hitting the Dallas clubs, sleeping late and ditching classes. Eric said the only weekend Brandon remained on campus was for the Freshman Follies, and otherwise he left campus each Friday evening and did not return until 5:30 or 6:00 on Monday mornings. Moreover, on some weeks Eric said Brandon left school on Wednesday evening, and in returning on Thursday morning would comment about "a wild party" in Dallas. The distance between Abilene and Dallas was 200 miles and a 3-hour drive on I-20, and Brandon was making the roundtrip trek twice a week.

Eric observed that Brandon's off-campus extracurriculars were interfering with his school responsibilities:

> Brandon would typically sleep during the days, I mean, especially Monday when he got back, he would sleep all day. He was more of a night owl. He stayed up during the night and slept during the day. So I knew he was missing a lot of classes. I would be up during the day, going to class and come back and he would still be in bed.

ACU had strict attendance policies which automatically drop a student from a class after four absences, and Brandon's disappearing act quickly caught up with him. Brandon was dropped from Intro to Ag and Systems and Tech on September 12, Finite Math for Applications on September 21, and English Composition and Rhetoric on October 7. He was down to an 8-credit course load which was considered part-time, and his prospects of meeting the attendance requirements for his remaining classes – let alone passing them – appeared poor. Brandon Woodruff was flunking out, and in all likelihood would not be returning for a second semester. In echoing the conditional acceptance set forth by ACU, Brandon's parents had told the boy that the first semester was the "last chance" to get his schooling together, and if he failed he would have to return home.

Brandon came from a solid middle-class background but his easy generosity, stylish appearance, and horse ownership led some of his ACU classmates to believe that his family was more affluent. Moreover, Brandon was a tad embarrassed about the old Dodge in which he drove around, and told many that his parents were giving him a new tuck if he proved himself academically. For example, according to Lindsey, Brandon "said his parents had bought him a new truck and he said that he was going to get that truck":

> I don't know the exact number but he mentioned it several times. He would go home on weekends to go get the truck. He would come back to Abilene with his same white Dodge truck, without the new one, and say, you know, his parents didn't want him to have it yet; they wanted him to prove himself with good grades and such things. And so that happened several times.

Eric similarly said Brandon often talked of getting a new Chevy:

> Fairly early on in the semester he told me his dad had bought him a new truck. He described the truck as a Chevy and was real excited about it, but there was always complications. He would go home every week and I'd say are you going to bring the truck back? Yeah. I'm going to bring it back. There were always complications.

Perhaps Brandon, a onetime shit-kicking hick, put on some airs and spent recklessly in an insecure desire to be accepted now that he was running with an affluent crowd in Dallas and attending a private college in Abilene. Such behavior is not so out of the ordinary. Who has not to some extent ever fudged their background just a little on a job resume or dating profile? Goodness knows what percentage of the Dallas population is keeping up with the Joneses and otherwise living beyond their means in order to prop up socio-economic standing in the public eye.

In addition to the money that Brandon earned from Chisholm Feed and Helix Studio over the summer he also financed his lifestyle on credit cards with which he was – like many students – a tad irresponsible. In July 2005 he obtained a CitiCard with a $2500 limit, and in just a one-week period from July 15 to July 21 maxed it out on clothes, electronics and restaurants, and then in mid-September acquired a Capital One credit card with a $1,000 limit which he maxed out by month's end. Tuition and board at ACU was expensive, and Brandon financed it through multiple sources including a $500 scholarship he received from the Rockwall County 4-H Club, a $7500 student loan he took out, and support from his parents. The 4-H scholarship supposedly caused a bit of a rift between Norma Woodruff and Norma Etherington, and the latter mama apparently thought her son Mike should have gotten it. When Brandon was dropped from some classes so early in the first semester for excessive absences he was issued a $1300 tuition refund, and of course the boy quickly spent it rather than turning it over to his father which resulted in a little row between them.

On the home front Brandon's parents were restructuring their financial affairs. The couple's combined salary was $125,000 a year – Dennis was making $70,000 at Flextronics and Norma was making $55,000 at Dal-Tile – and they also received income from a tenant leasing their land in Texarkana. However, money still was tight. Dennis only recently had started working again after losing his job at Alcatel. In the last few years he had been laid off multiple times from Alcatel, and after the final dismissal had an unemployment stretch. Dennis Woodruff picked up some gigs as a substitute teacher in the Rockwall schools which he enjoyed; however, he lamented the teaching pay and was relieved to get back into his technical field with the Flextronics job.

Over the years the Woodruff couple had accumulated $300,000 in personal debt on 30-plus credit cards. They always were generous with their children, and keeping horses in particular was an expensive pursuit. Now with both Charla and Brandon in college the Woodruffs were under greater strain. Charlotte Jackson met Norma Woodruff through Equest, and said Norma told her "that a lot of the debt came from the fact that Dennis and Norma always bought too many things for their kids" but they "always wanted the kids to do well, and hated to deprive the kids of anything." Brandon stated:

> Like I can honestly say, like, in my 19 years of, like, being with my parents, they, like – they were always there with us, like always. And like, if I was at a horse show or I needed them at 3:00 a.m. to wake up because I didn't feel comfortable with pulling a trailer, they were – you know, they were right there. Like, if I – I got into a bind, you know, moneywise, anything like that, they were there.

Brandon's comments reflect not only his parents' dedication but his own appreciation.

Dennis and Norma sought the help of a credit counselor, and then in September 2005 bought and moved into a double-wide manufactured home at 5545 County Road 2648 in Royse City in order to cut down on expenses. The new place was only 20 miles northeast of their Heath home, and it sat on five acres. The monthly payment on the Heath home was $1400, and only $500 on the trailer. Moreover, the real estate taxes would be substantially less on the rural property. The Woodruff couple was moving themselves with a load a night after work in Norma's truck and the stock trailer, and once that task was completed they planned to sell or rent the Heath home. The downsizing move may have been to cut expenses but Charlotte Jackson said country girl Norma Woodruff "was very excited about the new house and the fact that she would be able to have horses at the house" since it had more property, and she no longer would have to board them. The couple quickly began constructing a pole barn with four stalls. Although the new place was in a rural community it was not in complete isolation, and there were four houses directly across the street.

Charla Woodruff was in her junior year in fall 2005 at Southern Arkansas University in Magnolia which was a three-hour drive from her parents' new place in Royse City, and seemingly all was going well for the co-ed. She lived in a campus apartment with roomies Nicole Friday and Martha Thomas, was co-captain of a dance team and belonged to the Alpha Sigma Alpha sorority. She boarded her American Paint Horse at a nearby stable, and worked part-time at Magnolia Screen Printing.

The girl had a boyfriend, Jonathan Masall, who already had graduated from college and lived in North Carolina. When Charla went to visit Jonathan in North Carolina her overprotective parents insisted that she first provide them with a photocopy of his driver's license. Charla and Jonathan visited her parents for an overnight stay at their new place in Royse City during Labor Day weekend; however, the young lovebirds slept in separate rooms.

In mid-September Charla caught a nasty bug at school. The concerned parents came over from Royse City to attend to her at the Magnolia apartment. Although Norma Woodruff traditionally did not do a lot of housecleaning, Charla said that "mom went to Wal-Mart and bought a bunch of Lysol and mops and brooms and things to clean my apartment" – $200 in cleaning supplies – and over that weekend disinfected the place.

4 DOUBLE MURDER

On his weekend leaves from the ACU campus Brandon Woodruff typically would hit the Dallas clubs and parties at night, crash in his old bedroom at the Heath home, and during the day help out the folks at their new place in Royse City. The boy made no secret that he did not like either the double-wide or Hicksville, and had told his Aunt Linda "he would never live there and that he was never going to spend the night in that house." However, that did not hinder Brandon from being a dutiful son, and he helped his parents with settling into their new life.

On Friday night, October 14, 2005, Brandon once again headed out of Abilene for the weekend. He asked Adrienne Linge if she wanted to join him at a Dallas club but she had other plans. However, classmate Robert Martinez – described by Eric Gentry as "half Hispanic, half black, runs track, he's fast, athletic, a really good guy" – asked Brandon for a ride to Denton, a Dallas suburb, where his girlfriend Janssen Herring lived, and the easy-going Brandon readily assented. The two boys left ACU around 10:30 p.m. in the Dodge truck, and when they arrived at Janssen's place the ever-social Brandon stepped into her apartment for a quick introduction. Brandon told Robby he would pick him up Sunday evening for the return trip to campus, and then the boy left Denton to hook up with Alex Rulli and the plastics for some fun.

In the morning Brandon met up with his former girlfriend Morgan Lee. The old Dodge was temperamental again, and so Brandon first had dropped by his parents' place in Royse City to switch over to his mother's blue Toyota Camry as his weekend ride. Brandon reached Morgan's house on 1895 Creekside Drive in Rockwall at about 9 a.m. on Saturday. He was bearing gifts – some ACU souvenirs and breakfast from Sonic – for Morgan. As Morgan's mom Miss Lee stated: "[Brandon] probably knew that [Morgan] would wake up faster if she had food." After delivering his presents to Morgan in bed, Brandon went back downstairs. The boy chatted with Miss Lee while waiting for Morgan to get herself together, and Miss Lee said Brandon was quite candid about his ACU experience in stating that it "could be better and it's not going real great" due to his academic performance but otherwise "he loved it, had a lot of wonderful friends."

This was the first time Brandon had seen Morgan since the summer. Morgan said that when Brandon went to college their relationship "was kind of fading but we were still very good friends and talked a whole lot on the phone and – obviously weren't as relationship tight but still pretty good friends." The pair were hooking up this weekend because Morgan wanted help picking out a lamb for her 4-H project, and Brandon knew some people in Waco with good stock.

The two kids had a fun Saturday together particularly after all the obnoxious attempts over the summer and into the fall by Mike Etherington to drive a wedge between them with his busy-body mischief. By mid-morning they left Morgan's house in her truck for Waco, and then returned to Rockwall about 3 p.m. They also had dropped by Brandon's home in Heath before and after the Waco trip; first to get a cage for use in transporting the lamb, and then later to return the cage. After setting up the little lamb at the ag barn the pair returned to Morgan's house on Creekside Drive. Her parents had departed for the weekend to their cabin in nearby Poetry where they were overseeing construction of their new place. Brandon and Morgan took showers to wash away the animal funk. They hung out at the house for a few hours, and then about 10 p.m. headed to downtown Rockwall in Brandon's Camry to get some Chick-fil-A. Brandon had the misfortune of running into Mike Etherington at the fast-food joint which put him in a sour mood. Brandon drove Morgan back to her place. She got into her truck about 11 p.m. to join her parents in Poetry for the night, and Brandon hooked up with his gay friends in Dallas until about 3 a.m.

On Sunday morning, October 16, Brandon rolled out of bed in his old room at the Heath home, and drove to his parents' place in Royse City. In the late afternoon Morgan had returned from Poetry, and Brandon met her at the ag barn to check on the new lamb. He asked Morgan if she wanted to join his family for dinner – they were having pizza – but she declined the invitation, and Brandon headed back to Royse City. At six o'clock Dennis Woodruff left the house to pick up the pizza order from nearby Milano's, and he was back at 6:15 p.m.

Brandon ate a few slices and then left his parents' place sometime after seven o'clock in his Dodge truck. He headed to Serenity Stables operated by Tamara Keel at 700

North Sorrels Road in Royse City where the Woodruffs boarded their horses. Norma's Arabian had a skin irritation, and Brandon was going to bathe her with a Betadine solution. On his way there Brandon called Tamara who recounted their conversation as follows: "I told him to forget it because I'd already turned his horses out and he'd have to go catch her," and "Brandon said, well, that's fine, he'd have his mother do it later." However, Brandon still stopped at the stables in order to drop off the medication. The boy called his mother at exactly 7:36 p.m. according to phone records in order to relay the message about the horse but there was no answer.

From Serenity Stables the boy proceeded to the Heath home in order to feed the family pets which included two dogs, Jewel and Harley, two cats and a white cockatoo. In addition to feeding the animals Brandon also let the bird out of its cage, and he socialized a bit with his feathery friend. Brandon said that going from the stables to Heath was about a 30-minute drive, and taking care of the animals was perhaps a 30-minute task.

Norma's Silverado was on the Heath driveway, and hooked up to the stock trailer. Brandon said he had permission to take the Silverado back to Abilene because of some issues he was having with the old Dodge. In fact, on prior occasions Brandon had experienced roadside breakdowns with the Dodge truck when far from home, and his parents wanted to check it out rather than risking their boy again getting stranded along some desolate stretch of highway. No doubt Dennis and Norma Woodruff were overprotective about anything involving their children. Accordingly, Brandon swapped out his Dodge truck with his mother's Silverado.

It's unclear exactly what time Brandon left the Heath

home. On Friday night Brandon had told Robert Martinez that he would pick him up at his girlfriend's place in Denton on Sunday around 5 or 6 p.m. for their return trip to the ACU campus. That timetable already had been busted by Sunday's events, and around six o'clock the college buddies exchanged some calls in which Brandon told Robert that he was just sitting down for dinner with his parents, had some chores to perform and would pick him up in a couple of hours. Robert and his girlfriend were annoyed because Janssen was a student at North Texas, and she needed to study for a midterm exam the next day. Brandon still had not arrived when Robert called him at 9:49 p.m. to ask about the delay. Since Brandon was behind schedule he asked if Janssen could drive Robert from her apartment to a half-way meeting point. After a few more calls they agreed that Janssen would ferry Robert to Denny's at 9009 Skillman Road in North Dallas, off Exit 16 on Interstate I-635. Brandon rolled into the parking lot at Denny's about eleven o'clock where the impatient couple already was waiting in their car. In classic form Brandon was shirtless, barefoot and wearing designer shades behind the wheel of the Silverado truck.

Earlier in the evening Alex and Brandon had exchanged multiple telephone calls, including a couple about 9:30 p.m., to arrange for their usual Sunday night foray to Station 4. Once Robert hopped into the crew cab Brandon asked if he wanted to hit a Dallas club with some friends. Brandon did not come out to Robert but he did disclose there would be gay guys as well as straight girls at the hot spot. Robby was in an adventurous mood, and signed up for the outing. Robert asked Brandon why he was late in picking him up, and Brandon said he got "lost" along the way without any elaboration. Alex Rulli again was house sitting for his father in Plano, and Brandon and Robert reached the place about 11:30 p.m. James Britt also was at Alex's house, and they all had a beer while getting ready; as usual, Brandon barely drank half of his. Brandon gelled his hair and put on a shirt and shoes, and Robert ironed himself a fresh shirt. By midnight the foursome departed in Brandon's truck for Station 4.

Meanwhile, back at the Woodruff trailer in Royse City on Sunday evening, Dennis Woodruff called his sister Kathy Lach in Texarkana around 7:30. Kathy's understanding was that Brandon already had left his parents' place when Dennis called, and she recounted her brother saying "how Brandon had been out at the house helping him and Norma with moving in and getting everything organized and that they'd worked him pretty hard." In the call Dennis further told her about Brandon "liking boys." Kathy said that Dennis "did not sound angry at all" but "sad and caring is the way I would classify it":

> He seemed very sad and hurt and he said, I'm just so worried. And I said, what do you mean? He said, it's such a dangerous lifestyle. And I said, what do you mean, like HIV and AIDS? And he said, all of it, just the whole lifestyle. He said it was such a dangerous lifestyle. He was worried about his lifestyle and he was hurt for his son because he didn't want him going through any unnecessary misery.

About Brandon being gay Dennis emphasized "not that it's a bad thing but it's a more dangerous thing," and "we'll work through it."

Norma Woodruff then called her mother in Texarkana at nine o'clock, and they spoke about twenty minutes. Opal Johnston also said her understanding was that Brandon was not at his parents' home during this call. As it happened, Charla was visiting the extended family in Texarkana over the weekend, and was at her grandmother's when Norma called. However, Charla declined to speak with Norma, and said she would call her parents later that night upon returning back to SAU.

Charla left Texarkana at about ten o'clock, and an hour later arrived at her college apartment in Magnolia. She attempted to reach her parents at eleven o'clock but received no answer. Dennis and Norma Woodruff's three telephones – their respective cell phones and the home landline – were set up so that dialing any one number simultaneously would ring them all, and the first phone to pick up would receive the call and stop the ringing on the other two. Accordingly, Charla said it was "unusual for them not to answer the phone." However, Charla said she did not think much about it, and stayed up well into the night without trying again even though they otherwise spoke daily, and indeed, her parents specifically were expecting her call.

In Dallas at Station 4 Robert Martinez was a tad overwhelmed. He said "all the guys were dancing with guys and the girls were dancing with girls and I felt out of place," and he largely hung back as a wallflower. Robert noted Brandon's popularity at the club. The doorman exchanged hugs with Brandon, and let him in without charging cover. During the evening it "appeared that Brandon knew a lot of people there, and lot of people come up to talk to him" Robert said. Of course, Brandon spent a lot of time on the dance floor, and Robert still did not presume that his buddy was gay because "Brandon danced with some girls." However, Robert characterized Alex as "gay but didn't act like it," and James as "kind of fruity."

The four boys left Station 4 about two o'clock on Monday morning. Alex Rulli said Brandon "seemed perfectly normal" throughout the night and "didn't seem nervous or excited or stressed out about anything." Indeed, Alex continued, "nothing seemed out of the ordinary." Similarly, James Britt said Brandon "wasn't acting nervous or weird or strange or different in any way." However, an odd incident did occur on the ride from Dallas back to Plano.

Alex and James were in the backseat, and started rifling through Robert's bag. The silly queens pulled out his undies, and giggled out "whose are these? Aren't they cute." They then grabbed Brandon's bag, and as he was driving Brandon turned around and told them to knock it off. The consensus among everyone in the crew cab was that Brandon "freaked out." Brandon pulled the truck over on the highway shoulder, and he and James switched places. As James drove the remaining way to Alex's house Brandon sat in the back guarding over his bag. The next day Alex called Brandon in the early afternoon, and asked about the deal with the bag. Alex said Brandon told him it was gay porn "that he didn't want his friend Robert to see, and I understood and just kind of shrugged it off with that." Indeed, Brandon was not out to his classmate Robert, and ACU had strict policies against homosexuality. Brandon then texted to Alex "I'm sorry for flipping out. Wish we had more private time together. Have fun. Be safe."

Alex and James were dropped off at 2:45 a.m., and Brandon and Robby then headed from Plano to Abilene on I-20. They stopped at the Diamond Shamrock in Grand Prairie about four o'clock for gas and snacks – Robby had nachos, and Brandon lunchables – which Brandon charged to his

Capital One card. They arrived on the ACU campus two hours later. Tom Crews played baseball for ACU, and as he was going down the dorm stairwell between 5:45 and 6:00 a.m. for a team workout he passed Brandon walking up the stairs. As Brandon crashed his roommate Eric was getting up. Just another Monday morning.

After classes Eric Gentry returned to the dorm room about two o'clock in the afternoon, and by this time Brandon was up. Eric said "I didn't see a single thing different" about Brandon, and "he was still cutting jokes, cracking up." The two boys headed to the cafeteria with their friend Adrienne Linge for some lunch, and Adrienne too said Brandon was in his usual "good mood":

> And he was really talking about his truck and – and we all went to eat together in the Bean, which is the cafeteria at ACU, and he was really hyper and excited and he was dancing around in the cafeteria and singing and acting really silly. It was very amusing. He was playing the piano and singing and pretending like he was dancing and just being good ol' Brandon just goofy and fun.

Moreover, in telling folks about the Silverado truck, he made it clear that he had to return it to his parents which corroborated his statement that they lent it to him only on a temporary basis until the old Dodge was checked out. According to Lindsey "Brandon said when he brought it back his parents didn't want him to have it still because he needed to prove himself with like grades and stuff."

Meanwhile, at Southern Arkansas University in Magnolia, Charla attempted multiple times throughout Monday to contact her parents on their home, cell and work telephone numbers. Unable to reach them Charla said "I was very worried, very upset" and, quite simply, "freaked out." After a sorority meeting on Monday evening Charla then called Brandon about 7:30. She said "Brandon, I called mom and dad I can't tell you how many times," and he attempted to reassure his big sister: "It will be okay Charla. They're going to call me between 10:30 and 11. They always call me between 10:30 and 11. It will be okay. I'll call you." Eric Gentry was in the dorm room when Charla had called, and said Brandon relayed to him that "she couldn't get a hold of his parents." Eric told his roomie "your parents are probably just having some alone time or something, it's not a big deal. Don't worry about it, and Brandon was like 'okay.'"

After hanging up with Brandon, Charla went out partying on Monday night: "I went out, had a little fun with my friend." In further elaborating Charla said: "Charla got trashed. I got trashed." Stumbling back into her campus apartment in the wee hours on Tuesday morning Charla said she was unable to sleep because "then I remembered Brandon didn't call me," and "that's why I started panicking at 2 o'clock in the morning." Charla then launched into a drunk-dialing frenzy to her parents' phones: "I don't even care if I'm drunk. I can get through this. I can talk to them, I can talk to them like I'm sober. I called them repeatedly, repeatedly, repeatedly, repeatedly."

On Tuesday, October 18, Charla had no classes, and she again made multiple attempts to reach her parents. Their respective employers told Charla that Norma and Dennis had not phoned in. Around two o'clock in the afternoon Charla called Brandon to relay the ominous news about their parents' unexplained work absences, and Brandon in turn attempted to reach his parents from his ACU dorm. Eric was in the dorm room, and he recounted Brandon telling him "that's weird, I don't know where my parents are," and Eric said "I was just trying to calm him down, do the friend thing" by saying "well maybe they went on vacation, decided to take a break."

Finally, at about 3:15 on Tuesday afternoon, Norma's sister Linda Matthews in Texarkana called long-time family friend and Texas A&M extension agent Todd Williams to check on the couple. Williams worked out of the same building as Ron Merritt, the Rockwall County Health Coordinator and a volunteer fireman, and together the pair went to the Woodruffs' Royse City home. There was no answer when they knocked, and all the doors and windows were locked. The men popped out a screen and pried open a window, and a stench hit them which Ron immediately recognized as decomposing bodies. Inside Todd and Ron found the obviously-slain couple, and they quickly exited the trailer to call police who arrived about 4:30 p.m.

The married couple was sitting close together on a sofa before the television, and both had been shot and stabbed multiple times. Dennis was shot once in the face, and had nine stab wounds, some as deep as five inches, to his face, neck and upper torso; Norma was shot three times in the face, and had a four-inch front-to-back gash across her neck. Norma was turning into Dennis as if for protective cover, and Dennis held in his rigid hand a chewing tobacco spit cup. Their clothes and the sofa were blood soaked. The television was on but all the lights were off, and the cardboard box on which the TV sat had blood splatter.

The firing was done from just inches away as indicated by the tight patterns of dark soot and red stipple on their skin surrounding the bullet entries. The medical examiner characterized "soot" as "a very fine smoky material" that "comes out of the gun when it's fired," and is "the product of combustion that are occurring from the actual flame in the barrel of the gun." And "stippling" is "the actual particles of gunpowder that strikes the skin and cause tiny injuries, burns or abrasions, from these burning or unburned particles of gunpowder that come out and hit the skin."

The single bullet to Dennis Woodruff entered on the left side of his mouth where the lips meet, took out multiple teeth, went through the tongue, perforated the throat and finally lodged in the number two cervical vertebrae. The medical examiner stated "the bullet didn't actually go into the cord" but "into the bone right next to the cord," and "there's going to be a significant amount of concussive-type force associated with the bullet being that close to his cord." The number two cervical vertebrae is "very high up in the cord," and the bullet impact "would cause him to be unable to breathe and it would also cause him to be paralyzed" but "not necessarily unconscious," and that injury alone would have caused his death within "seconds to minutes."

His nine stab wounds "all had hemorrhage associated with them" according to the medical examiner. Wounds one and two were on the left side of Dennis's face, and one was 2 ¾-inches deep hitting the carotid artery and jugular vein which "is going to bleed profusely and that injury also in and of itself is potentially rapidly fatal injury." Stab wounds three through five were characterized as "cluster wounds that are very close together" on the right side of the face, and the deepest one was 5 ¾-inches into neck musculature. Wounds six and seven were in the soft tissue on the back of the neck, and the deepest one was two inches. Wounds eight and nine were around the right armpit, and the deepest one was 5 ¼-

inches. The medical examiner could not determine the order in which the stab wounds were inflicted but "they all happened probably about the same time," and "he was alive during all of them but I can't tell you exactly what order they happened in."

Norma was shot three times. The first bullet hit the back of her hand at the base of the index finger – presumably a defensive wound as if she reflexively was cowering in a vain attempt to protect against the firearm – and then travelled into the right side of her face. A second bullet also hit the right side of her face. The medical examiner said the two bullet entrances on the right side of the face "were so close together that I couldn't separate their paths" as they continued "through the right maxilla, the upper part of the jaw with fractures, the tongue and the second cervical vertebrae body in the midline of the upper back of the neck." Both bullets exited "at the left upper back of the neck" – one "behind the left ear and below it," and the other "a little further back from that" – and "each one of those was probably a lethal gunshot wound." The third bullet entered through the left cheek, knocked out teeth, exited under the left side of the chin, and then re-entered the body to lodge in the collarbone. This bullet "may have gone through the tongue" but "it was harder to tell because the tongue was already hit by numbers one and two." The poor woman further had a four-inch gash along the left side of her neck, and the knife entered at the lower front and then moved along towards the back in a slightly-upward path before exiting.

The couple had been living out of boxes in their ongoing move from the Heath house to the Royse City double wide, and there was some clutter in their new home.

Valuables in plain sight such as televisions, computers and jewelry were not taken. There was a trail of so-called "cast off" blood – presumably dripping from the knife or killer – from the living room into the guest bathroom. The shower had visible moisture "in the corners, the soap dish, where water collects and it had not dried yet" suggesting that perhaps the killer cleaned up. All the locks on the front door including the safety chain were in place which indicated that the perpetrator left through the side door to the car port which had been locked upon departure.

Linda Matthews received the bad news from Todd Williams about five o'clock on Tuesday afternoon, and she relayed to Brandon and Charla that their parents were dead. The surviving family had not yet been advised that Dennis and Norma were murdered but as word spread folks naturally assumed foul play. Brandon was in his dorm room at ACU when he got the call from his Aunt Linda, and Eric Gentry said the boy responded with "uncontrolled weeping" on his bed: "He loses it. He's just bawling. Rolling all over the place. He was bawling when he found out. Just devastated." Robert Martinez also was in the dorm room at that moment, and he similarly observed that "Brandon cried like he missed them, you know, like any other kid would have. He showed a lot of emotion. He started crying real bad."

Brandon insisted on flying rather than driving home, and his friends accompanied him to Abilene Regional Airport. Tim Applewhite described Brandon as "really upset" and "crying" at the airport, and Eric Gentry said he was "shaking, bawling." The last commercial flight to Dallas already had left, and over the phone Michelle Lee used her credit card to arrange a $2,000 charter plane for Brandon. Miss Lee and Morgan met Brandon at Love Field airport in

Dallas, and on the car ride to Texarkana where the grieving family was gathering Brandon slept in the back seat with his head on Morgan's lap.

In Texarkana, Brandon stayed with his Aunt Kathy who was Dennis's sister, and Charla stayed with her Aunt Linda who was Norma's sister. The closed-casket funeral was on Saturday, October 22, and officiated by John Cannon and Micah Mauldin to reflect both the Church of Christ and Baptist traditions on the Woodruff and Johnston sides of the family, respectively. Brandon's friends from ACU – Eric Gentry, Tom Crews, Adrienne Linge, Tim Applewhite and Lindsey Ferguson – travelled down to support him, and brought the Silverado truck. Brandon apparently was taking Valium over the weekend provided by his Aunt Kathy, a nurse at Christus St. Michael Hospital, to handle the stress. During the funeral services Brandon closely clung to Morgan.

5 HASTY ARREST

Texas Ranger Jeffrey Collins pulled the laboring oar in the murder investigation with assistance from the Hunt County Sheriff's Office. The Rangers are a division of the Texas Department of Public Safety headquartered in the capital city of Austin, and largely investigate major felonies. They are organized into six companies with operations throughout the state, and in murder cases a Texas Ranger typically works alongside the local sheriff. In 2005 Collins was assigned to company B which had an office in the same building as the Hunt County Sheriff's Office at 2801 Stuart Street in Greenville, TX. Jeffrey Collins was 21-years-old when he started his law enforcement career with DPS in 1989, and over three decades has served as a state trooper, narcotics investigator and Texas Ranger. His father had been a Ranger, and Jeff joined that storied division in September 1998. Ranger Collins currently heads the public integrity unit in Austin.

The investigative team quickly made several assumptions based on the crime scene. There was no forced entry and no signs of any struggle. Accordingly, Collins quickly concluded that the Woodruff couple likely was surprised by the attack as they sat on the sofa watching television, and only someone whom they trusted could engender such vulnerability. Moreover, given that the place was not ransacked and no valuables were taken, robbery was ruled out as the motive. Instead, Ranger Collins said "the murders of the victims were consistent with the suspect being enraged at the victims and nearly all the trauma caused by the shooting and the stabbing of the victims was directed at the head and necks of the victims." He said the perpetrator proceeded with a "personal cause" in light of the vicious overkill at such immediate proximity which involved attacking them with a knife even after their likely deaths from the shooting. Collins said "the injuries, especially the stab wounds to Dennis, made it a very personal homicide, a very personal cause homicide." In light of the crime scene Ranger Collins concluded that the killer "is going to be somebody that is close to the victims."

In 2014 cable network Investigation Discovery produced an episode about the Woodruff murders dubbed "Lone Star Mystery" for its series *Nightmare Next Door*. Among those interviewed was Sgt. Noel Martin from the Smith County Sheriff's Office who also participated in the investigation, and he said the killer specifically had an issue with Dennis rather than Norma due to his greater injuries from the post-mortem knife assault. Sergeant Martin said the killer had a "personal issue with Dennis for some reason and Norma just happened to be in the way." Norma "happened to be at the wrong place at the wrong time," Martin continued, and the killer's rage clearly was directed against Dennis "where he just wanted to continue to take his aggression or anger out on Dennis just wanted to overkill – keep killing Dennis."

The investigative team entertained a passing suspicion that perhaps the horrible crime involved a love triangle in some way. Although a robbery motive had been quickly eliminated, Dennis's wedding ring – a plain gold band – was missing, and no one had an explanation for its disappearance although he otherwise was known to wear it. Moreover, numerous multi-colored condom packets were strewn about the couple's bedroom floor, and Dennis's porn collection was in plain sight. The prominence of the sex-related material and the missing wedding ring prompted investigators to question whether the Woodruffs were swingers or otherwise having affairs, and perhaps their killer was a jealous lover or humiliated cuckold. Perhaps the killer stole the wedding ring in a symbolic gesture believing Dennis Woodruff had dishonored his marriage? However, law enforcement came up empty-handed in their inquiry into this angle just as the Woodruff couple had once shot down their daughter Charla with her accusations about marital infidelity. The Woodruffs were a happily-married couple according to all accounts, and devoted only to each other.

The spit cup in Dennis's hand was another inexplicable detail at the crime scene. Investigators surely were surprised that Dennis did not lose his grip on the spit cup during the brutal onslaught, and even more surprised when the autopsy report showed no indication in his mouth that he had been chewing tobacco. Accordingly, the real possibility existed that the killer placed the spit cup in his hand after the murder. Dennis did not chew every day, and usually there was a spit cup around the house which was not regularly emptied. The investigators simply did not know what to make of the missing wedding ring, the visible porn collection, the strewn condom packets and the tobacco spit cup. Was the killer staging the crime scene to expose Dennis Woodruff and his vices, and provide some explanation for his murder? In the end, all which could not be explained simply was cast aside by investigators.

By Thursday, October 20, just two days into the investigation, Ranger Collins considered Brandon Woodruff the prime suspect, and then arrested him Monday morning on October 24. The boy still was staying with his Aunt Kathy at her Texarkana home, and in the early morning a SWAT-like team rousted him out of bed from his sleep. "It was really shocking to me," Brandon said. "They told me they were charging me with the death of my parents, and I was just like no, no, no. The louder I got the more they didn't listen." Nevertheless, Brandon immediately waived extradition, and a police caravan transported him from Arkansas over the state line into Texas where he was processed and detained in the Hunt County Detention Center in Greenville which adjoined the same building out of which the Sheriff's Office and Texas Rangers operated. As Brandon succinctly put it: "plucked out of reality and put into a county jail cell."

Incredibly, law enforcement had no physical or other direct evidence tying the teenager to the horrible crime: no murder weapons, no bloody prints, no eyewitnesses, no confession The investigators literally had nothing, and were proceeding pursuant to little more than a speculative hunch. Indeed, shortly after his arrest, Ranger Collins expressly admitted that "we're not saying at this point we got proof beyond a reasonable doubt at all" which would be necessary in order to convict Brandon Woodruff for his parents' murders.

Jeffrey Collins was personally guided by a deeply-held Christian faith which he openly shared during witness interviews throughout the investigation. "I like going to church," he said, and told witnesses that he was an ordained elder. In his interview with Dennis Woodruff's sister Kathy Lach, conducted on October 26 just two days after Brandon's arrest, Ranger Collins paraphrased verses from the Book of Proverbs teaching that parents must warn their children about the consequence of the death penalty for committing murder:

> I tell parents you need to go to the first proverbs. Solomon wrote this wisdom thousands of years before Christ. He lays out a capital murder in the first psalm. He tells his son don't be enticed by sinners and when they tell you let's lie in wait for someone's blood and we'll split up the purse don't do it because it will cost you your very life. And I tell parents you need to be teaching your kids that right now because your kids may not be a victim, they may be on the other end of that if you don't teach them that right now.

Ranger Collins already was urging Kathy Lach and the surviving family to pray for the poor boy's eternal soul:

> The good thing about Brandon is even if he did it he can still be forgiven. You know what I mean? What's here, this world right here, doesn't matter because it's temporary. It's the eternal thing that we need to be concerned about. He can still do that you know but he's going to have to confess and repent, you know, and I mean that's the conditions. If Brandon did this

just because he did that doesn't mean that he can't be saved. That's why he needs the family. If the family loves him, you know, besides coming down here and visiting, you need to be praying for him, you know, all the family needs to be praying for him and they need to be praying for themselves too because it's only through the Holy Spirit that you'll be able to fully forgive somebody, you know, we're not made to do that really, the human side of us it's hard for us to forgive.

Brandon just had been arrested without any physical evidence, and the lawman already was sending the boy straight to hell.

Ranger Collins presumably also adhered to traditional Christian fundamentalist beliefs that homosexuality is a sin. In speaking with witnesses he did not refer to Brandon as "gay" but as living an "alternative lifestyle." Although Collins repeatedly said this "alternative lifestyle" did not matter to him from a policing perspective he did let it slip out in one witness interview that "I don't understand" how "it's kind of a cool thing now," and then in another interview groused about how the societal trend to protect gays from discrimination was undermining religious freedom.

Few people believed that Brandon Woodruff murdered his parents, and immediately upon his arrest some surviving family members questioned whether Ranger Collins had considered Brandon's sister Charla in the investigation. Kathy Lach told Ranger Collins during her October 26, 2005 interview that between the two siblings "I just have this weird gut feeling but I just know if I had to choose Brandon would not be who I would choose." In elaborating, Kathy said she knew each child's "case histories and personality," and Charla "has reason to dislike and be jealous because she did not get attention" whereas "Brandon got a lot of attention." Moreover, given Charla's criminal justice studies, she has "more knowledge about the system and know how to work it." Indeed, Kathy Lach seemingly attributed a "mastermind" intelligence to Charla by which perhaps the wannabe cop even could direct an accomplice to perform the dirty work:

> Two people could be involved together, and one being the mastermind, one being the smart person . . . one collecting the money and one mows the grass, you see what I'm saying? I just want to get that off my chest.

Kathy Lach further warned Ranger Collins that in meeting with Charla Woodruff to "pay attention to the tone of her voice and dialect" because there is one which is "calm and mature and grown up," and then there is her manipulative "baby talk" with which she draws the unsuspecting into her web.

Indeed, Charla's appearance in her videotaped interview with Ranger Collins on October 23, 2005 was a tad disturbing. The young co-ed generally comported herself in an infantile manner by speaking in a soft tone and hugging herself. However, other times she came across as a creepy flirt with silly giggles and hair twirling.

There were moments when it appeared as if Charla were projecting herself onto Brandon. For example, after discussing her slain father's supposed raging history, Ranger Collins asked Charla "who took after your dad when it comes to that – you have the temper or your brother has the temper?" Incredibly, Charla pointed to Brandon. Ranger Collins used this statement from Charla in his sworn affidavit the next day to secure an arrest warrant based on probable cause against Brandon Woodruff for his parents' murders: "Charla Woodruff also indicated that Dennis Woodruff underwent electroshock therapy when she was a child for anger management and his explosive temper. Charla Woodruff indicated that Brandon Woodruff inherited their father's temperament." However, friends and family repeatedly characterized Charla as the sibling with the family conflicts and anger issues. After all, it was Charla who once physically assaulted her father and had attempted suicide multiple times. Brandon was described by many witnesses as the easy-going spirit who typically backed away from confrontation let alone initiate it.

Perhaps the oddest moment during Charla's videotaped interview was when she attempted to laugh off the physical assault against her father a few years earlier. She explained that they were in the hallway, and she made a running charge at him. However, Charla said that her father was so big that she simply bounced off him and fell to the floor on her ass. Charla started giggling before Ranger Collins to emphasize the absurdity of such a little girl as herself taking on such a big man as Dennis Woodruff; however, her parents at that time were sufficiently concerned by Charla's out-of-control behavior that they called the cops to the house over the incident even if charges ultimately were not pressed.

Throughout the interview Charla repeatedly emphasized how "big," "huge" and "strong" her father was. Indeed, at one point Charla suggested she could not be his killer given their size disparity. Ranger Collins asked Charla "do you know of anybody that was close to your parents that could have the capability of doing this?" She raised a hand from her lap, and pointed it at her chest as if being accused.

"The thing is," she said, "me against my dad?" She then emphasized her father's size by continuing as follows: "I tell you. Whoever did this had to be huge or strong. He's huge. Huge. I'll tell you that. I mean. I don't understand. I mean. I really don't understand. Our dad is a very big man."

Charla could not let go of the issue, and during the remaining interview frequently came back unprompted to her father's imposing size. For example, about thirty minutes after the Ranger's question about anyone with "the capability of doing this," Charla said the following:

> It doesn't make sense. Do you know how big my dad is? My dad is a huge guy. He's six-foot – and he's a big guy. Because I'm telling you my dad is a big guy. Nobody I know is that big. None of it makes sense to me at all.

And then fifteen minutes later said the following:

> I just don't understand. Maybe the door was unlocked and somebody came in as they were sitting on the couch. I just don't understand how – unless someone is just so huge they can gain control of the scene and tell them to just stay there. Because my dad's big and a very strong guy. It's not like he's so huge that he can't move.

Yes, Dennis Woodruff was a big man. However, even the biggest man can be controlled with the point of a gun, and it's curious how Charla did not consider that possibility even if the surviving family had not yet been told that a firearm was involved with the murders. After all, that's the beauty of firearms: they're great equalizers. That concept inexplicably seemed to elude the otherwise highly intelligent Charla who was a third-year criminal justice major with an eye for a police career. Indeed, just a year earlier Charla Woodruff had expressed her "fascination with guns" and "the authority or the power" of being a cop. So surely Charla should have understood the killer really did not need to be "so huge" in order to "gain control of the scene."

It wasn't just Kathy Lach who asked Ranger Collins if he considered Charla Woodruff during the murder investigation. Heck, Collins told Kathy "you don't need to think that you're the only person who's thought that." On November 20, 2005 the Ranger held a meeting with the family members, and he said "the purpose of the meeting was to sit the family down and to explain to them what evidence has been collected against" Brandon. At the end of the meeting Bonnie Woodruff "became extremely agitated," and she stated "that the investigators had been focused on the wrong suspect," and with Brandon's sister in the room the grandmother came right out and said "she thought that Charla Woodruff needed to be looked at more closely" and "Bonnie WOODRUFF even asked Charla WOODRUFF where she (Charla WOODRUFF) was on the night of the murders."

Todd Williams also thought that Ranger Collins may have acted too quickly in arresting Brandon Woodruff, and suggested that the lawman consider administering a polygraph examination to Mike Etherington in light of the falling out between the two boys among other reasons. However, Collins did not look kindly upon Todd for the unsolicited advice, and seemingly threatened the poor man with an investigation upon unfounded suspicions from an unidentified member in the Woodruff family that maybe the 4-H advisor had turned Brandon gay through an inappropriate relationship. According to Todd Williams there were "a lot of intimidations and an accusation" from Ranger

Collins, and "one of the accusations was that he had received information that there was a possibility of me having inappropriate relationship with Brandon." Collins fully admitted in his investigative report that he "informed Williams that information had come in to investigators early on in the investigation that suggested that although Williams was a married man, Brandon Woodruff's choice of a homosexual lifestyle may have been brought on by Williams' close relationship to Brandon Woodruff." In fact, there was no evidence that Williams ever was sexually involved or otherwise inappropriate with the boy. Todd thought the entire investigation had been an incompetent endeavor in its myopic focus on Brandon Woodruff as his parents' alleged killer, and he said the Ranger "was not really interested in other options of what might be possible," and "really tried to intimidate me." Todd further said "I had never been interviewed and I thought that just from – there was probably information that they might need that they had not thought about."

Brandon had concerns as well about Mike Etherington in light of the bad blood following their breakup in spring 2005, and he relayed them to Ranger Collins. Mike was oddly obsessed with Brandon's sexuality and relentless in gossiping about him, and Brandon told the Ranger in his interview on October 23 about threatening messages he allegedly received only weeks earlier from his friend-turned-nemesis:

> About two or three weeks ago at about eleven o'clock, I got a text message saying, "I've grown up a lot in high school. You don't know who you've messed with. Remember my name – Mike Etherington. You're going to need it one day." Well,

that was followed by about 16 to 18 text messages until four o'clock in the morning. Just different things, like, you know, my parents are white trash, I was white trash, all this, you know – and that's why I printed out the text messages. Because even for my girlfriend's sake, like I just wanted to know. And I called my girlfriend. I said, "Would you please call Mike and tell him to please quit text messaging me?" I said please. And it went until four o'clock, until I turned my phone off.

Notwithstanding his suspicion Brandon nevertheless reserved judgment on any role his onetime friend Mike Etherington may have had in the double murders: "Am I going to say that I know a hundred percent that he did it or that I don't think he did or whatever? I don't know, because I have five hundred questions that I don't know. You know?" Among the questions Brandon had was "I still don't even know how my parents died." Although law enforcement had disclosed they were murdered, as of October 23 when the Woodruff children were interviewed the actual means still were under wrap.

Ranger Collins assured folks he had looked at Charla Woodruff and Mike Etherington but that the evidence simply did not point to them as the killers. However, Collins ultimately was no big fan of Mike Etherington. Immediately after news was released on October 19 that Norma and Dennis Woodruff were dead but before it was known publicly that they had been murdered, Mike's mother Norma Etherington – Mama E as Charla Woodruff liked to call her – called the Hunt County Sheriff's Office. The investigative report provides the following: "Investigator Gibson received a phone call from a lady who identified herself as Norma

Etherington," and "during Brandon Woodruff's senior year he began to separate from his friends and began dressing differently" and "there were rumors Brandon Woodruff was leading an alternate life style, and he hated his parents." Norma had heard this information from her son, and accordingly, law enforcement spoke with Mike Etherington who eagerly dished about Brandon Woodruff in a seeming effort to paint him as likely responsible for his parents' deaths.

Ranger Collins liberally used Mike's statements in his supporting affidavit for probable cause to secure an arrest warrant, and among the factual representations in the court filing were that Brandon Woodruff had written hateful comments about his parents on his MySpace page:

> Michael Etherington stated to investigators that on a web page utilized by Brandon Woodruff, Brandon Woodruff stated that he "Hated his fucking parents and wished they were fucking dead." Etherington went on to state that Brandon Woodruff indicated on the web page that his parents were losers and never did anything for him.

However, Mike later admitted to the Ranger that he personally never saw any such written comments but only heard about their supposed existence from someone else who purportedly once had read them, and later the investigators were not able to find on the MySpace server that the comments ever existed in the first place.

Upon hearing the changed story Ranger Collins said "I hate to tell you this Mike but I'm just about ready to strangle you," and he ripped the young punk a new asshole:

> That information was very matter of fact first-hand knowledge and that's not what you're telling me right

now. Documents were prepared that I sweared to that this information came across to us. There's nothing I can do about that now. I swore to the fact that that's what I believed was true and correct. You don't understand what kind of a bind that really puts you in for providing that information but this is not a good thing. You provided information to investigators that was used as part of probable cause to where [Brandon's] sitting in a jail cell right now. I got a problem. I got a huge problem with that. I don't necessarily have a problem with what has happened because there's other probable cause and yours may not have been needed to do that.

The Collins affidavit included other allegations which "Etherington informed investigators he had personal knowledge of about Brandon Woodruff" but again much turned out to be based on rumor and hearsay from others.

Ranger Collins was warned that Mike Etherington had credibility problems. For example, Michelle Lee specifically told the lawman that he should not necessarily believe what Mike said about Brandon because there was bad blood between the two boys. Unfortunately, Ranger Collins simply parroted Mike's claims without independently corroborating them for purposes of getting an arrest warrant against Brandon Woodruff. Moreover, after learning that Mike did not have "personal knowledge" of the dirt he was dishing, Ranger Collins should have disclosed to the court that the arrest warrant was issued pursuant to a tainted affidavit. Although Ranger Collins believed "there's other probable cause" to support the arrest warrant and Mike's allegations "may not have been needed to do that," this conclusion was not for him to make; instead, the Ranger should have given the court the opportunity to revisit the issue. Indeed, it was a "huge problem" as Ranger Collins aptly noted, particularly since the supporting affidavit did not cite any direct evidence against Brandon Woodruff. The boy sat in a jail cell as law enforcement kept from the court pertinent knowledge that undermined the arrest warrant it had issued.

Ranger Collins asked Mike Etherington about his whereabouts on Sunday evening, October 16. Mike said he attended a church function with his girlfriend that let out at 6:45 p.m., and then he hung out at her house in Rowlett until 9:30 p.m. when he left for home apparently after receiving a telephone call from one of the shit kickers. Mike lived with his mom at 711 Breezy Hill Lane in Rockwall, and said once there at ten o'clock he took a shower and was in bed "lights out" by midnight or 12:30 a.m. However, his phone records show that he made a 142-second call at 2 a.m. on Monday, October 17, which originated from a cell tower only five miles from the Woodruff trailer in Royse City. Of course, Mike very well still could have been at home and in bed. After all, the Etheringtons lived only ten miles on a direct route from the Woodruff couple – they were almost neighbors now – and so any call Mike made from his home probably would connect through a cell tower so close to the Woodruff place. But one thing appears certain from the phone records: Mike Etherington certainly did not sleep straight through the night.

Although Ranger Collins ultimately gave Mike Etherington a cold shoulder he apparently gave Charla Woodruff a warm embrace. Some family and friends of the Woodruff family suspected that under the Ranger's wing Charla fancied herself as Nancy Drew on the case, and there were frequent calls between the two. Jeff Collins even may have helped Charla Woodruff realize her childhood dreams of becoming a police officer according to some conjecture.

In October 2005 when Norma and Dennis Woodruff were murdered Charla was in her third year at ASU as a criminal justice major; however, her suicide attempts including once with a firearm would be a red flag – if not an automatic disqualifier – for many law enforcement agencies. Only a year after the horrible crimes Charla Woodruff obtained a coveted job as a criminal investigator with the Miller County Sheriff's Office in Texarkana, AR. There was some speculation that Ranger Collins helped secure her the MSCO position even while she was serving as a government witness in the ongoing investigation against her brother. Moreover, Charla Woodruff in her interview with Ranger Collins had provided him with a detailed account of her suicide attempts. A long-time friend of the Woodruff family said "it is my understanding that the Texas Ranger guy got Charla the job in Miller County," and further elaborated that at least some relatives were so shocked given her past behavior that they apparently confronted the then-Sheriff: "I do know that the family went to the Sheriff and told him that they were concerned and scared for her to be carrying a gun and driving a sheriff's car," and "the sheriff apparently cut them off and said she was a great employee and they were not going to change anything."

The "minimum standards" for becoming a certified peace officer in Arkansas are established by the state's Commission on Law Enforcement Standards and Training (CLEST), and Regulation 1002 requires, among other criteria, that all applicants be examined for emotional stability by a licensed psychologist "who after examination find the officer to be competent and recommends the agency hire the individual." The parameters for this "psychological examination report" are defined under Specification S-7 which recognizes that "the emotional stability to withstand the pressures of modern law enforcement work is an essential qualification for applicants for law enforcement service and although psychological tests and interviews have recognized limitations, many personality defects can and are identified through screening by trained professionals."

The criteria established by the CLEST under Regulation 1002 and Specification S-7 for becoming a certified law enforcement officer in Arkansas do not expressly address suicide attempts by an applicant. In Arkansas "any certified law enforcement officer . . . may carry a concealed handgun" under statute 12-15-202 but anyone who has "threatened or attempted suicide" is barred from obtaining a license to carry a concealed handgun under statute 5-73-309. However, statute 5-73-309 applies only to civilians and not police, and so individuals who have attempted suicide such as Charla Woodruff may carry a concealed handgun by going into law enforcement. It's unclear whether this loophole was intentional or an oversight by lawmakers, and arguably a suicide attempt should be an automatic disqualifier for a police applicant for the same reasons that a suicide attempt is an automatic disqualifier for obtaining a concealed carry.

The CLEST criteria only are "minimum standards," and Regulation 1002 expressly states that "higher standards are recommended whenever the availability of qualified applicants meets the demand." However, it's unclear whether the Miller County Sheriff's Office had additional standards beyond the CLEST minimum at the time Charla Woodruff obtained employment. Perhaps Brandon Woodruff's lawyer Jerry Spencer Davis said it best at an October 26, 2006 pretrial hearing before Judge Beacom: "Charla Woodruff by the way, now is a criminal investigator for the Miller County Sheriff's Department, strange, strange."

The state may not have suspected Mike Etherington and Charla Woodruff for any role in the horrific murders but at trial in March 2009 the defense team floated their names. However, the trial judge shut down questions about Charla. Although she admitted in open court before the jury that she once attempted suicide with a firearm in high school Judge Beacom would not allow defense lawyers to cross-examine state witness Linda Matthews – Norma's sister – concerning that and other related issues. The defense lawyers proffered that they wanted to "demonstrate that Charla Woodruff reported that she had a bad relationship with her parents," and "the identity of or the motives of individuals who may have had reason to want Norma and Dennis Woodruff dead is relevant." Moreover, the defense argued that since "the murders occurred with a firearm," it wanted to explore further "that Charla had experience with firearms and knew how to use a firearm."

The state was successful in getting Judge Beacom to preclude this cross-examination as a "feeble attempt" by the defense "to suggest that [Charla] had anything to do with this." However, whether the defense effort was a "feeble attempt" goes to the weight rather than the relevancy of the evidence, and arguably Judge Beacom should have afforded the defense team wider latitude in exploring alternative narratives particularly given the weak evidence against Brandon Woodruff. Indeed, the prosecution's argument of a "feeble attempt" is ironic given that its own case against the boy was so weak. Shouldn't what's good for the gander be good for the goose?

The state was adamant that all the evidence pointed to Brandon rather than Charla or Mike as the killer, and at trial Ranger Collins testified "frankly, I didn't believe that any – that the evidence showed that [they] had anything to do with it." A decade later Investigation Discovery produced an episode about the Woodruff murders dubbed "Lone Star Mystery" for its series *Nightmare Next Door*, and among those interviewed was Ranger Collins. He made it clear that investigators had looked at both Mike Etherington and Charla Woodruff which involved pulling their phone records, interviewing them and checking out their alibis. With respect to Brandon's sister Ranger Collins concluded that "all of the information together put Charla Woodruff in Arkansas at the time of the murders." And then with respect to Mike Etherington, Ranger Collins concluded the investigation "put him where he said he was which was not around the crime scene during the time period that this took place." It appears that the state's elimination of Mike and Charla as potential suspects revolved around its assumption that the double murders were committed on Sunday at about 9:30 p.m. rather than perhaps later that evening or even into early Monday.

6 PROBABLE CAUSE?

Upon Brandon's arrest Ranger Collins conceded "we're not saying at this point we got proof beyond a reasonable doubt at all" which is the legal standard for a criminal conviction. That's an understatement. There was absolutely no physical or other direct evidence linking the boy to his parents' murders. However, the lawman believed he had "probable cause" for an arrest warrant even though the supporting affidavit largely was cobbled together with hearsay gossip and questionable claims from Mike Etherington and Charla Woodruff. The deciding factor for Ranger Collins in moving to arrest Brandon Woodruff was a faulty timeline that the boy provided in recounting his whereabouts for Sunday evening, October 16, after having pizza with his parents.

The funerals for Norma and Dennis Woodruff were on Saturday, October 22, in Texarkana, AR, and the following day Brandon voluntarily travelled to the Hunt County Sheriff's Office in Greenville, TX for an interview jointly conducted by Jeff Collins from the Texas Rangers and Terry Jones from the HCSO. During the funeral Brandon was doped up on Valium according to multiple accounts, and it's unclear whether he still was taking the powerful sedative on the day of his police interview.

Norma's sister Linda Matthews worked for thirty years as a legal assistant at Autrey, Autrey & Stewart in Texarkana, AR, and she arranged for father-and-son lawyers LeRoy and Wren Autrey to attend the interview with Brandon. Although just a three-man shop it was politically connected. Ned Stewart had been city attorney for Texarkana Board of Directors since 1993 for which he received a monthly retainer, and Wren Autrey became a Miller County District Judge in 2008. LeRoy Autrey, now deceased, characterized himself to Brandon "as your temporary attorneys, and as such, we are bound by our – by the law and our professional ethics. We can't repeat anything that's been said in here." Linda Matthews told Brandon going into the interview "to tell the truth," and "as far as we knew he was one of the last ones to see" his parents alive, and the police "were going to question him hard."

Ranger Collins told Brandon that "this is not a custodial interrogation" and "you're free to leave at any time." However, LeRoy Autrey inexplicably twice told the scared 19-year-old boy in front of the lawmen that there may be adverse consequences against him for not answering questions, and the statements seemed more like a coercive tactic against an uncooperative witness rather than sound advice to a purported client. As the interview began LeRoy Autrey told Brandon "if there's any question that you don't want to answer, of course, you have a right to remain silent" but "on the other hand, they have a right to have you arrested and put you – you know, charge you." And then to underline the point again repeated "you have a right not to answer" but "on the other hand, there are consequences of not answering, and we can't – we can't guarantee that – that something won't happen." Frankly, it seemed that LeRoy Autrey was doing a better job advancing the interests of law enforcement rather than protecting the rights of Brandon Woodruff. At one point he even told Brandon "not to argue with the officer," and "that's the best professional advice I can give you." And then again: "My advice is not to argue with the officer." The boy was visibly frightened like the proverbial deer in the headlights, and at one point in speaking about the overwhelming tragedy of his parents' murders and their burial blurted out "I've got like a broken glass right now, and I don't know what piece to pick up, because there's so much."

Terry Jones fancied himself a weekend cowboy, and at the interview's start dissed Brandon after learning of his success in the horse world for not looking like a normal wrangler: "Well, if you don't mind me saying, the horse thing, you just – I rope and everything, and you just didn't look like –" Brandon interrupted Jones to explain that he had been "doing, like, portfolio work and stuff" and over the last six months had dyed his hair multiple times. The cowboy-hat-wearing Terry Jones just did not know what to make of the flaming teenage boy. After Brandon advised that he was a student at ACU Jones commented "that's kind of rough for somebody that's a party guy."

During the interview Brandon visibly was moved by his parents' murders, and told investigators "I don't know how any human could do something" like this. "I think a freak would have to do this," Brandon said, and "I don't know how any human is possibly capable of taking another human's life. I think it's unnatural." In response, Ranger Collins concurred and referenced his own Biblical touchstone: "I agree with you a hundred and ten percent that it's not natural. But you go all the way back into Genesis with Cain and Abel. It started then and it hasn't stopped now."

Under questioning Brandon laid out his whereabouts for Sunday evening. Brandon stated he left his parents' Royse City house sometime after seven o'clock although "I can't say an exact time." He dropped off a bathing solution for his mother's horse as corroborated by the stable owner in Royse City, and then called his mother at 7:36 p.m. but there was no pickup as confirmed by phone records. Brandon told investigators he then went to the Heath home to feed the family pets. The drive from Royse City to the Heath home takes "at the most" thirty minutes, and to feed the animals takes "at the most" another thirty minutes Brandon said. He switched out his Dodge truck with his mother's Chevrolet, and then headed for Denton – typically a 45- or 55-minute trip – to pick up Robert Martinez. Ranger Collins asked Brandon "so you think probably by eight o'clock, then, you're headed towards Denton" to which the boy simply answered "yeah."

In getting Brandon to agree that he "probably" left Heath for Denton by eight o'clock, Ranger Collins believed he had caught the boy in a lie about his whereabouts. A few days earlier on October 20 Ranger Collins had interviewed Randall Lunz, the Woodruff neighbor in Heath, and Lunz told Collins that on Sunday evening, October 16, he woke up sometime after ten, got out of bed to look out his window, and saw Brandon on the driveway. It's unclear exactly what time he spotted the boy. Randy said he typically prepares for bed once the ten o'clock news comes on, and his usual routine – letting out the dogs and brushing his teeth – takes from ten to twenty minutes. However, that Sunday was not a usual day. Randy and his wife were exhausted from the horse show they attended. In fact, Mrs. Lunz retired earlier than normal, and Randy said he was "trying to get to bed as close to ten o'clock as possible." He looked at the clock when he went to bed but only generally recalled that it was "shortly after ten." In light of the sighting Ranger Collins suspected that Brandon did not directly go to the Heath home from the stables in order to feed the family pets. Instead, Ranger Collins theorized that after dropping off the Betadine solution at Serenity Stables the boy returned to his parents' place in Royse City, killed them, and then proceeded to the Heath home where he was seen by Randy Lunz a bit after ten. However, this was not the "gotcha moment" Ranger Collins believed it was, and his speculative thesis simply does not withstand scrutiny for multiple reasons.

In short, Brandon simply was wrong about the time, and much of the responsibility for that mistake lies with the faulty interrogation by Ranger Collins. The lawman did not simply ask Brandon what time he left Heath for Denton but instead asked a leading question in which the departure time expressly was planted, i.e., "so you think probably by eight o'clock, then, you're headed towards Denton." Leading questions are not allowed on direct examination in court proceedings precisely because they suggest a specific answer, and accordingly, do not have the same evidentiary value as an open-ended question which allows the witness to answer based on his own independent recollection. Brandon's gratuitous assent to the leading question from Ranger Collins is particularly meaningless because the frightened boy already had been told by LeRoy Autrey "not to argue with the officer."

Moreover, Ranger Collins had erroneous assumptions

in calculating the eight o'clock departure time which he planted on Brandon Woodruff. The lawman accepted that it took thirty minutes to drive from Royse City to the Heath home, and thirty more to feed the family pets; accordingly, Ranger Collins concluded that Brandon necessarily must have left for Denton by 8:00 p.m. However, this reasoning presumes that the boy left his parents' double wide trailer in Royse City after dinner precisely at seven o'clock and headed directly to the Heath place. This assumption by Ranger Collins simply is not supported by the undisputed record. Brandon told the Ranger he left the double wide sometime after seven o'clock but "I can't say an exact time." Moreover, Brandon did not go directly to the Heath home; rather, he proceeded to Serenity Stables where he dropped off the Betadine solution, and telephone records establish that he made a 7:36 p.m. call to his mother to relay a message from Tamara Keel that the horses already were out to pasture. Accordingly, Brandon probably did not even arrive at the Heath home until sometime after eight o'clock given the 30-minute ride from the stables in Royse City.

Ranger Collins also incorrectly presumes that once at the Heath home all Brandon did was feed the pets for thirty minutes, and that he did not spend additional time occupying himself with other activities. For example, Brandon also swapped out the trucks with the stock trailer on the driveway which was not accounted for by Ranger Collins. And who knows what else the boy was up to while at the Heath home? Once again, incompetent questioning by Ranger Collins is to blame. Brandon did not even purport to represent that caring for the pets was an exhaustive list of all his activities, and the Ranger's failure to ask if there were anything further in which he had been engaged was a rookie police interrogation mistake.

For example, it appears as if Brandon perhaps had a wank at the Heath home, and understandably that was not something the teen boy just volunteered to his interrogators particularly since he was not pressed to identify all his activities while there. When the investigators executed their search warrant for the Heath home on October 22 among the seized items was a light blue red-trimmed shirt on Brandon's bed. They sent the shirt to the lab thinking it may be a smoking gun since Brandon was shirtless when he arrived in Denton to pick up Robert. However, the lab did not find his parents' blood on the shirt; rather, it found Brandon's semen. The teen boy wasn't knocking off his parents during this time; rather, he apparently was whacking off himself. Indeed, Robert Martinez told Ranger Collins that when he impatiently called Brandon at 9:49 p.m. to inquire about the pickup delay it sounded like "he was having sex or something" or "just had sex." The semen-stained shirt on Brandon's bed at the Heath home, his shirtless arrival in Denton and Robert's statement all suggest that Brandon did not just feed the animals. Sure, the gay boy only was nineteen, and the act may have taken only a few minutes, but maybe he nodded off after the climatic shoot for an indeterminate period which even Brandon could not accurately recollect? Who knows how long the boy may have been whacking off, and the point simply is that Ranger Collins failed to ask Brandon to account for all his activities at the Heath house before departing for Denton.

Brandon was just off with his time in agreeing with the Ranger that he "probably" left Heath for Denton at eight o'clock. The Ranger's question was in leading form and contained faulty assumptions, and Brandon's half-assed "yeah" is probative of nothing. The boy did not even have a knack for time. For example, when Ranger Collins kept repeating that Brandon left the Royse City trailer home at seven o'clock on Sunday evening after the pizza dinner, the boy replied "I can't say an exact time," and when Ranger Collins asked him what time he got back to the college campus on Monday morning Brandon said "I don't know. I really don't."

Multiple witnesses were off by an hour or two in recounting their times, and there was no suggestion they were lying but simply had made honest mistakes. For example, Alex Rulli and James Britt both independently said Brandon and Robert arrived in Plano at 10:30 on Sunday evening when in fact it was an hour later. And Robert Martinez was even worse than Brandon with time. During his November 2, 2005 interview with Ranger Collins an obviously nervous Robert said he received a call from Brandon on Saturday, October 15, but "I'm not really sure what time he called." Even when Ranger Collins asked if he could narrow the call's time to just "Saturday afternoon or evening" Robby only could answer "I'm not really sure what time it was but I remember him calling me Saturday." Robert repeatedly was off by an hour or two on the Sunday events including when calls were made or received or when people arrived or departed. Ranger Collins specifically asked "could you be a little off on these times," and Robert responded: "Yes, sir. I could be off. I wasn't tracking the time. I didn't keep up with the time. Most of the times were guesstimated."

Even Randall Lunz had trouble in recounting a precise timeline for his own events over that weekend. For example, he said on Saturday he twice saw Brandon and Morgan in the driveway at the Heath home. The first time "it was mid-morning, somewhere between 10 and 12, I would say," and "then around 1 o'clock, 2 o'clock when I saw them again." And Randy attended a horse show with his wife on Sunday, and recollected getting back that evening between five and six o'clock, and then had dinner "probably about 7. Somewhere, 7, 8."

Recollecting time can be a funny thing, and being off by an hour or two is not unusual. When people don't have reason to keep track of time, they usually don't. After all, people typically do not mark exact times as inconsequential events casually unfold in their ordinary course, and looking back to accurately re-create that timeline is nearly impossible as Alex Rulli, James Britt, Robert Martinez, Randall Lunz and Brandon Woodruff all discovered. As Brandon later said: "Everything I told that Ranger I was honest about. I was just off on my times, and that doesn't make me a cold-blooded killer."

Brandon's bad sense of time was surpassed only by his bad sense of direction. Although Ranger Collins was incredulous that Brandon could have gotten lost on Sunday evening going from Heath to Denton to pick up Robert – they eventually met about eleven o'clock at a half-way point in a Denny's parking lot – none of Brandon's friends were surprised. As Miss Lee aptly stated, Brandon was a "goofy fart." The kid had problems with directions even in getting to places where he previously had driven. For example, during the interview Ranger Collins asked Brandon "where does [Alex Rulli] live at over in Plano," and in true form Brandon answered:

> Plano west. I don't know. I have to get directions all the time, because I always get lost every time. I ended up driving on the wrong side of the road because in

those Plano streets and you don't know where you're going and all those lights are all messed up.

Similarly, after Brandon told the Ranger that on Sunday night the group left Alex's place to go dancing at Station 4, the following exchange occurred between the two:

Q. And that's in Dallas. Is that like in the West End area or where? Where is that in Dallas?

A. I don't even know.

Q. You don't?

A. No. Because they were like – like, Alex showed me how to get there. Because I was with Alex, James, Robert and me.

Brandon was not putting on an act, and multiple witnesses corroborated that the teenage kid easily got lost when driving. For example, Alex Rulli told Ranger Collins that "I do know [Brandon] needed some actual directions to get to my dad's house." Similarly, when Ranger Collins asked Eric Gentry about Brandon's apparent capacity for getting lost, the long-time friend and college roomie expressly said "it seemed normal that Brandon could get lost." Robert also told Ranger Collins that on Friday night when driving from ACU to Denton Brandon in fact got lost: "He got lost. Then we had to call my girlfriend and ask directions. We took the wrong turn and then we had to turn back around."

Brandon Woodruff's failure to precisely recall the time he left the Heath home on Sunday evening to pick up Robert Martinez from his girlfriend's in Denton did not constitute probable cause to issue an arrest warrant particularly when there was no physical evidence tying him to his parents' murders at their home in Royse City. It's an attenuated stretch; a bridge too far. It's not even circumstantial evidence; it's just unfounded speculation. Not only does the record demonstrate that Brandon Woodruff simply was off with his times, but the state's proffered timeline on when the boy supposedly murdered his parents does not logically compute.

If Brandon Woodruff murdered his parents then he had only a narrow timeframe in which to do it according to the state's own calculations. Norma in Royse City got off the phone with her mother at 9:20 p.m., and Opal Johnston's understanding was that Brandon was not even there at that time. Randall Lunz saw Brandon on the driveway in Heath shortly after 10:00 p.m., and it's a 30-minute drive from Royse City to Heath. So whenever the boy re-appeared at the double wide – assuming he ever did – Brandon had little time to shoot and stab both parents multiple times, and then eliminate all physical evidence tying him to the crime.

Frankly, a professional hit team and clean-up crew could not proceed as efficiently as Brandon purportedly did. The police looked everywhere – the two homes, Brandon's dorm room, all the vehicles – but were unable to find the murder weapons or any item linking the boy to the crime. The lab did not find any blood from the boy's parents on any of his clothing, the bracelet he was wearing, or the vehicles he drove. There were no bloody shoeprints or fingerprints from Brandon Woodruff anywhere. And the suitcase over which Brandon was so protective on the ride back to Alex's house from Station 4 on Sunday night? The lab detected absolutely nothing in it: no gunpowder trace, no Woodruff blood. Apparently, Brandon was telling the truth about the suitcase, and he just wanted to keep his friends from finding the porn; after all, even Brandon's gay friends did not know about his adult work, and the boy certainly did not want it disclosed to ACU classmate Robert Martinez. Ranger Collins just could not accept the simple fact that the evidence did not point to Brandon Woodruff, and with his myopic focus on the gay boy misinterpreted every innocuous or otherwise readily-explainable event with a sinister connotation which time-after-time never played out.

The speculative theory spun by law enforcement about Brandon's whereabouts was unnecessary. In fact, the evidentiary means existed by which to establish rather conclusively his exact location during the period between seven and ten o'clock on Sunday evening. Sadly, the incompetent investigators never obtained this critical evidence. In this time frame Brandon made and received several calls from and to his mobile phone. The carrier maintained records of the geographic locations for the cell towers through which every call connected, and could have pinpointed where Brandon was for each one. However, the investigators overlooked acquiring the relevant records for Brandon's account in order to place his actual whereabouts.

Brandon had a Cingular Wireless account which investigators subpoenaed, and yet the records inexplicably showed no usage on Sunday, October 16, between 3:06 a.m. and 10:46 p.m. The investigators were perplexed because cross-referencing the records of others showed that Brandon had made and received numerous calls throughout Sunday including during the critical period. Kirk King, a deputy marshal from the technical operations group within the U.S. Marshal's Office who specialized in using cell towers and phone records for geographic tracking, said "there were some calls that were made by the defendant that were showing up on other people's cell phone records but not his own." For example, Brandon made a call to his parents' Royse City home at 7:36 p.m., made one to Alex Rulli at 9:28 p.m., made one to Morgan Lee at 9:32 p.m., received one from Morgan at 9:41 p.m. and received one from Robert Martinez at 9:49 p.m.

It turned out that Brandon's calls were connecting through the cell towers of AT&T Wireless which Cingular Wireless recently had acquired. The two providers maintained separate networks but their respective towers were accessible for each other's customers, and in order to get a complete picture of Brandon's phone activity the records from both companies had to be subpoenaed. Jerry LaBerteaux, Directory of RF Engineering for AT&T Mobility, explained it as follows:

At the time in 2004, Cingular Wireless purchased AT&T Wireless, and at that time we had two separate networks. There was an AT&T Wireless network and a Cingular Wireless network. And when we completed the acquisition, we allowed all Cingular customers to access the AT&T wireless network and make calls and then, vice-versa, all of the AT&T wireless network could access Cingular wireless network and make calls. They would be transparent to the user. So the assumption I would have to make, not having the AT&T Wireless phone records, would be that he was actually on the AT&T Wireless network instead of Cingular Wireless, which is very logical and I have seen that many times in the past, during that period.

Although Brandon's call data was not showing up on the subpoenaed Cingular records, LaBerteaux said "it would have been available from the AT&T billing system"; however, those AT&T records had been purged by the time investigators discovered the reason for Brandon's missing calls in his Cingular records.

Frankly, the failure of law enforcement to acquire this key data which would have conclusively established Brandon's whereabouts through the tower locations should have resulted in a dismissal of the indictment. The investigators had the opportunity to establish his actual whereabouts but they instead presented nothing but conjecture after dropping the ball. How convenient for the state now that potentially exculpatory evidence was forever gone. Moreover, even though the phone records from other people conclusively established that Brandon Woodruff was on his cell phone during the short period in which law enforcement insisted the boy otherwise was engaged in a brutal rampage against his parents, that phone never was even tested for their blood.

Ranger Collins made one other assumption which perhaps was misplaced in cobbling together his speculative theory that Brandon Woodruff squeezed in a double murder on Sunday evening, October 16. When Randall Lunz saw Brandon Woodruff on the Heath driveway shortly after 10:00 p.m. his parents – thirty minutes away in Royse City – very well still may have been alive. There is no hard evidence on when Norma and Dennis Woodruff actually were murdered, and since it's unlikely that Brandon could have done it within the narrow window as insisted by the state perhaps they were killed later that Sunday night or even early Monday morning.

The couple certainly was alive by 9:20 p.m. when Norma Woodruff finished talking with her mother Opal Johnston on the telephone, and Ranger Collins just assumed they were dead by 11:00 p.m. at the latest because neither answered the phone call from their daughter Charla Woodruff. However, just because someone does not pick up the phone does not mean they're dead. Heck, even Charla said she did not think much about it when her parents failed to answer, and she otherwise stayed up well into the night without calling again. Moreover, just like Charla should have understood that someone can control a huge guy like Dennis Woodruff at the point of a gun, Ranger Collins should have understood that someone brandishing a firearm can order a captive couple not to answer the phone.

The state's own medical examiner was unable to establish a precise time when the Woodruff couple was murdered. "It's really difficult to tell exactly what [their] time of death was," she said, because determining time of death based on decomposition is "not an exact science." Although it was "a possible scenario" they were killed on Sunday, October 16, it also was "possible it could have been a little longer than that or a little bit shorter than that as well" including early Monday on October 17. Curiously, on Tuesday evening, October 18 when investigators examined the crime scene, the guest bathroom still had water "in the corners of the shower, the soap dish, where water collects and it had not dried yet." Moreover, although the area was rural, there were four houses directly across the street from the Woodruff trailer. The neighbors were home on Sunday evening but none of them heard anything. If Brandon Woodruff fired off four gunshots around 9:30 p.m. in the quiet countryside surely the neighbors in close proximity would have heard. Maybe the murders happened much later that night or into the wee morning hours when the neighbors were in deep slumber and would not hear anything.

There was no probable cause to arrest Brandon Woodruff because there was no evidence against him. Brandon Woodruff overwhelmingly was described as a fun-loving, good-hearted soul, and yet Ranger Collins – relying largely on trash talk from Mike Etherington and Charla Woodruff – transformed the boy through a questionable affidavit into a criminal mastermind who cunningly planned to kill his parents, and in a nearly-impossible tight period carried out the double murder, eliminated all physical traces of his involvement at the grisly scene and disposed of two weapons. And then went dancing. That's rich. The boy could not even get his act together to attend classes but now supposedly had carried out the crime of the century in northeast Texas? Heck, if Brandon were intent on murdering his parents that weekend why did he invite Adrienne Linge to go clubbing that Friday night? Why give Robert Martinez a ride with the promise to pick him up on Sunday for the return trip? Why ask Morgan Lee to the Royse City double wide on Sunday for a pizza dinner? In short, why introduce so many last-minute variables that could queer the plan? God bless the ditzy twink but Brandon Woodruff was no mastermind.

Upon his arrest Brandon Woodruff was charged with capital murder for his parents' deaths in Trial Cause No. 23,319, and arraigned in the 354th District Court in the Hunt County Courthouse in Greenville, TX before the Honorable Richard A. Beacom, Jr. Beacom attended Catholic University in Washington, D.C. on a full scholarship, and graduated with an economics degree in 1966. He then received a law degree in 1969 from University of Texas, and signed up with the U.S. Army where he served as a captain for four years with the Judge Advocate General's Corps which serves as legal counsel for the military. Beacom's father was a World War II veteran, and participated with the Army Air Corps in the Normandy Invasion. After an honorable discharge in 1973

Beacom and his family moved to Greenville where he maintained a private practice until 1997 when elected to the bench. The Catholic faith had an enduring role for Judge Beacom, and he was an active parish member of the St. Williams Catholic Church, and a Grand Knight of the Knights of Columbus council.

The Hunt County District Attorney's Office assigned ADAs Noble D. Walker Jr. and Keli Aiken to prosecute the case against Brandon Woodruff. Walker was a local boy, and graduated from Greenville High School in 1981. He received his undergraduate degree in history and literature in 1988 from East Texas State University, and three years later in 1991 obtained his law degree from St. Mary's School of Law in San Antonio. Walker served in the U.S. Air Force from 1985 to 1986 as an administrative specialist with the 3486th Civil Engineering Squadron, and then was an air cargo heavy equipment operator with the Texas Air National Guard from 1986 to 1992. Most of Walker's career after law school was as a local prosecutor although he had a five-year stint in private practice which included representing the city of Greenville on municipal matters. In 2009 Walker was elected as the Hunt County District Attorney, and still maintains that position. Keli Aiken was just a greenhorn in October 2005. She had received her law degree only a few months earlier in May 2005 from Texas Wesleyan University. Aiken remained with the DA's Office until 2017 when she succeeded Judge Beacom on the bench upon his retirement. In the judicial election Aiken ran as a Republican, and she easily defeated her Democratic opponent by garnering sixty-four percent of the vote.

In Brandon Woodruff's murder case Judge Beacom appointed Jerry Spencer Davis as his defense counsel. Davis received his law degree from Southern Methodist University in 1970, and was a former District Attorney for Greenville. Davis immediately filed motions challenging the "unlawful incarceration" due to the "absence of probable cause," and in the alternative, challenging the $1,000,000 bail as "excessive and prohibitive" both of which were summarily denied.

In setting bail the judge is supposed to consider whether the defendant is a public threat or a flight risk, and neither of these factors were implicated in Brandon's case. The murders of Norma and Dennis Woodruff supposedly involved a "personal cause," and so even under the state's own theory Brandon Woodruff did not remain a threat to anyone else even presuming his guilt rather than innocence. Brandon did not have a criminal record or violent past, and he hardly was some wild boy ready to tear up the community. Brandon also was not a flight risk. He had multi-generational ties to the community on both sides of the family, and his grandmother Bonnie Woodruff agreed to take custody over him. Mrs. Woodruff poignantly told the court: "I loved my son and daughter-in-law very much but I know that Brandon did not do this" as "he loved his parents very much and they loved him also." Moreover, even if released on reduced bail, the government could require that Brandon wear an ankle bracelet for electronic monitoring.

In the week after Brandon Woodruff purportedly murdered his parents and before his arrest the boy engaged in no behavior which remotely suggested that he was a public threat or flight risk. At the end of his interrogation on October 23, Ranger Collins pretty much directly accused Brandon Woodruff of murdering his parents, and the boy was adamant with his denial: "I'm telling you a hundred percent. No. That's fucking crazy. Excuse my language."

And yet after the interrogation Brandon Woodruff did not skip town but instead went right back to his Aunt's house where the next morning police rousted him out of bed, and the boy even agreed to waive extradition to allow his transport over the state line from Arkansas to Texas. Under evidence rules flight is an indicia of guilt but Brandon Woodruff did not flee even after Ranger Collins told him he was in the law's crosshairs.

At his bail hearing the court gallery was filled with row after row of family, friends and neighbors, and they all stood up "in support of Brandon receiving a lower reasonable bond based on their knowledge of him." Multiple letters were filed with the court on his behalf from 4-H members, church leaders and business owners attesting to the boy's character. For example, Ede Bullock, a family friend and Brandon's employer at the Chisholm Feed Store, "would trust him with anything we did" including the care of her children. Robert B. Fry, an elder at the Walnut Church of Christ which held the funeral services for Norma and Dennis Woodruff, found "it inconceivable that this lad could have perpetrated an horrific crime of the magnitude thought and brought to this court."

Courtney Shlensky, a friend with whom Brandon became close in his senior year of high school after he parted ways with the shit kickers, wrote a long from-the-heart letter to Judge Beacom in which she described Brandon Woodruff as both a goofy and sensitive boy including the following:

> He truly has touched my heart. He always had open arms for me to fall into and ears for listening to me when I needed someone to talk to. He was always there for me many times when no one else was there for me. I very rarely saw Brandon in a bad mood. If

he were he would be in a good mood after 10 minutes. Also, if I were in a bad mood or had a bad day it wouldn't take but 5 seconds for Brandon to make me laugh and put a big smile on my face. Brandon being so much fun to be around, something in my everyday life reminds me of him and just makes me laugh. Sometimes when I'm in a bad mood or it's a bad day I wish Brandon were with me to make my day better. Over all Brandon has changed my life in such a positive way. He has taught me not to worry what people think about me, to just be me and goofy.

There was not a single witness who spoke against Brandon Woodruff at the bail hearing.

Judge Beacom was unmoved by the public support for the teen boy. Indeed, the jurist did not even consider the public threat and flight risk – or lack thereof – with respect to the individual defendant before him as clearly required by the case law, and instead Judge Beacom candidly admitted that he just treats all those accused in capital murder cases in the same way. From the bench Judge Beacom stated "in reviewing the bonds in other capital murders, finds that $1 million is pretty much the norm," and "I've got five or six other people in jail with similar charges at $1 million." Of course, as defense counsel Jerry Davis pointed out, the defendants in all those other cases had prior convictions, and 19-year-old Brandon had none. Moreover, there was no physical or other direct evidence in the case against him. It did not matter. In a one-sentence order Judge Beacom denied the request for bail reduction, and provided no explanation for the decision: "After reviewing the file, the request for a bond reduction in the above numbered and styled cause is denied."

Unable to make the ten percent or $100,000 to post the $1,000,000 bond, Brandon Woodruff remained behind bars for the next three years awaiting trial clinging only to hope that someday the truth would set him free:

> I really felt like the truth would come out. For a long time I didn't even think I would go to a trial. I just thought they'll find out the truth. It wouldn't even be an issue. There would be no trial, there would be no court hearings.

Brandon was in the belly of the beast.

7 DIRTY TRICKS

The state was in a desperate panic. It had charged Brandon Woodruff with capital murder but by its own admission did not have sufficient evidence to convict him at trial. Indeed, there was absolutely no physical or direct evidence. Lacking conviction in their own case the prosecutors went low, and resorted to a shameful series of dirty tricks ranging from constitutional violations to a smear campaign in an unconscionable bid to make the flimsy charges stick against the teen boy.

From the moment that Brandon Woodruff was locked up both Ranger Collins and ADA Keli Aiken eavesdropped on his telephone conversations including those with defense counsel. The Hunt County Detention Center records inmate calls for security purposes, and a pre-recorded message on the phone system disclosed this at the start of each call. Normally, the recorded conversations are automatically erased within ninety days; however, Collins and Aiken made an exceptional request to Curtis Neel, the Chief Jailer at the Hunt County Sheriff's Office, to turn over Brandon's recordings for their own use. The Ranger and the

ADA in the aggregate listened to hundreds of Brandon's recorded telephone conversations preserved on multiple CDs over varying periods from his initial incarceration in October 2005 through July 2007 when the defense team inadvertently found out about this unseemly practice.

Given the warning at the start of each call perhaps the police snoops as a general matter were entitled to obtain Brandon's recorded telephone conversations without a court order, and arguably his privacy rights under the Fourth Amendment were not violated. However, that's a debatable proposition since there was no disclosure the recorded calls could be turned over to law enforcement for purposes unrelated to jail security. More fundamentally, however, among the calls which were being recorded and monitored were those between Brandon and the entire defense team including attorney Jerry Spencer Davis, his legal assistants and the court appointed investigator involving case preparation, factual development and witness assessments. This was a clear violation of Brandon's right to effective assistance of counsel under the Sixth Amendment independent of any privacy right under the Fourth Amendment. The Texas legislature even had codified this Sixth Amendment principle to require that correctional facilities "shall ensure that no confidential attorney-client communication is monitored or recorded." Under well-established case law this constitutional right cannot be deemed waived by an inmate simply because a jail discloses that calls are subject to monitoring. The inmate must converse over the telephone with his attorney in preparing a defense, and he has no choice but to use the system provided by the jail. An inmate has the right to presume that his attorney-client communications remain protected from law enforcement even if aware that his other calls are subject to monitoring.

Jerry Davis was outraged upon discovering that the prosecution team was listening to his telephone conversations with Brandon Woodruff, and there was an outcry among many high-profile practitioners from the defense bar in Hunt County. Edgar J. Garrett, president of the Hunt County Bar Association and a Professor of Criminal Justice at Texas A&M University, stated "I was not aware that the Hunt County Jail recorded phone calls for security purposes, and I certainly was not aware that attorney/client phone calls would be monitored and recorded and then shared with the Hunt County District Attorney's Office or other law enforcement agencies." Garrett further concluded that "as a Professor of Criminal Justice, I believe this practice violates an inmate's rights under the Constitution of the United States of America." Smith E. Gilley, a former Assistant County Attorney for Hunt County and six-term member of the Texas House of Representatives who sat on the Criminal Jurisprudence and Judicial Affairs Committee and the House General Investigating Committee, stated the snooping "smacks of Watergate," and is "despicable and simply wrong." Similarly, Peter I. Morgan, a former County Attorney for Hunt County, said that "I never at any time during my tenure as Hunt County Attorney ever requested the Hunt County Jail to monitor and record attorney/client phone calls, or have the recordings of such phone calls turned over to me for use in prosecution against the defendant," and "it is my opinion that such actions by the prosecuting authority would be in violation of a defendant's [constitutional] rights."

Jerry Davis secured the appointment of Katherine A. Ferguson as co-counsel to spearhead a challenge against the prosecution team for its gross intrusion into the sacrosanct attorney-client relationship. Ferguson received a B.A. in English from Texas A&M in 1988, and got her law degree in 1991 from Texas Tech University School of Law with numerous honors. For many years Ferguson had a varied practice including civil matters, financial services and family law, and only in the late 1990s began picking up criminal defense work. On August 29, 2007 the defense team filed a motion to dismiss the indictment for violating "the Attorney Client Privilege which safeguards a defendant's right for effective assistance of counsel for advice, trial strategy and defense preparation" under the Sixth Amendment.

In a courtroom hearing Ferguson pointedly called out the telephone eavesdropping as a desperation tactic by the prosecution team due to its weak case against Brandon Woodruff:

> The only reason they listened to these tapes and didn't tell anybody about it, there can be only one reason, they were hoping to get a leg up. They were hoping to get access to how Mr. Davis and Mr. Woodruff and other members of the staff, how they perceived the relative strengths and weaknesses of the State's case and how they perceived the relative strengths and weaknesses of their own defense, what witnesses they might call, whether or not Brandon would testify. That's an important right, right there. That knowledge if they discussed that. This goes to the entire process. It is inextricably intertwined with the entirety of this case. It goes to everything. They can have gained information that will allow them to

make decisions about what jury members, what potential jurors they might want to call, based on what they glean as their possible defense, now they know and can make decisions in jury selection, say, well, we know who the defense is going to call so we want to look for jurors that are going to be sympathetic to this kind of defense or a witness, strategies for attacking witnesses.

In short, as Ms. Ferguson rhetorically asked, "if they've got their case so sewn up and so wrapped up that they're so confident about it, then why is Keli Aiken asking for the tapes?"

The constitutional challenge was a slam dunk for the defense lawyers, and Judge Beacom ruled on September 17, 2007 "that the practice of the State listening to a defendant's telephone conversations with his attorney is a violation of the 6th Amendment," and that "Mr. Woodruff's 6th Amendment rights have been violated." Of course, Ranger Collins and ADA Aiken were caught with their hands in the proverbial cookie jar, and the judge really could not have reached any other conclusion without appearing like a complete tool for the government team. However, Judge Beacom refused to dismiss the indictment because it found Brandon did not suffer any "prejudice" from the violation; in other words, no harm, no foul.

In order to show prejudice Brandon Woodruff had to point to a specific instance where the state gained a meaningful advantage in the case arising from its surreptitious activity. However, the evidence by which the defense could demonstrate that prejudice was kept from them. Ranger Collins said he had taken "handwritten notes" on the calls he heard but "tossed them" after claiming "they were of no value to me" because "I never saw those tapes as evidence." ADA Aiken preserved her forty-six pages of handwritten notes on fifty hours of telephone conversations but the presiding judge refused to allow defense counsel either to examine her or see the notes on the ground that it was work product which reflected upon the prosecution's case. Of course, as the defense aptly pressed, that precisely was the point: only the handwritten notes that ADA Aiken made in listening to conversations between Brandon and his attorney would reveal whether she garnered an unfair advantage to the defendant's prejudice in preparing for the trial. The only way to determine what Aiken learned was actually to examine what Aiken learned, and that was contained in her forty-six pages of notes on the telephone conversations; however, this obvious principle eluded Judge Beacom, and he fully protected the state. As Katherine Ferguson vainly had argued before Judge Beacom:

> We can't even find out what they may have heard or what they may have thought about it because you wouldn't let me put Ms. Aiken on the stand. How can I demonstrate prejudice if I can't talk to the very people who are prosecuting the case to find out what they heard, what they learned and what they did about. I can't prove prejudice if you won't let me question them about it.

Judge Beacom's inexplicable protection of Aiken and her notes from examination necessarily precluded the defense team from showing the prejudice the judge required them to show in order to dismiss the indictment.

The entire proceeding had a Kafka-esque absurdity: the Constitution supposedly guarantees rights to a defendant but the government only is held accountable for violating those rights upon a showing of prejudice, and then the defendant is denied access to the evidence by which to show that prejudice. The United States proudly may tout its justice system but Katherine Ferguson was challenging Hunt County as a banana republic in arguing that the only remedy for the pervasive Sixth Amendment violations was an outright dismissal of the criminal indictment against Brandon Woodruff:

> At some point there has to be a respect for the Constitution. This has been a gross intrusion into his privilege by the State of Texas, not only by the Sheriff's office, but by the Rangers, and specifically by the Hunt County District Attorney's Office. When there is such a gross intrusion, there's only one remedy, Your Honor. Because there is only one way that any citizen in this county is going to be able to think that we have a legal, fair, and equitable adversarial system that protects everyone's rights. Otherwise we might as well say we're in some banana republic. But it's actually worse than if we were in a banana republic because here we're trying to put a veneer of, well, it's legal and it's okay on it to just violate fundamental rights. He has an absolute right to confer in private with his attorney. It has tainted the entire proceeding.

The court refused to dismiss the indictment after finding that the government violated Brandon's Sixth Amendment rights because Brandon Woodruff was unable to point to any prejudicial taint.

Nevertheless, Judge Beacom believed some remedial measures were required, and ruled that "any evidence obtained from any telephone calls placed by Mr. Woodruff to members of his defense team is suppressed" and "any evidence obtained as a result of investigation from information obtained from such phone calls is likewise suppressed." Judge Beacom appointed Webb Baird, a visiting judge from Paris, Texas, to examine the prosecution file including its handwritten notes on the recorded conversations. However, this suppression review was conducted in a secret proceeding – known in legal terms as *in camera* – at which the defense lawyers were not allowed to participate. Criminal justice in the United States is supposed to be an adversarial system, and yet Brandon's own advocates who knew the case better than anyone were excluded from providing their insight and advocacy during this crucial proceeding. Who knows what Judge Baird may have missed in sifting through the prosecution file to ensure the exclusion of all fruit from the poisonous tree. The judge may have allowed material to remain which the defense would have argued should be eliminated. So Brandon had his Sixth Amendment rights violated twice: first, by Ranger Collins and ADA Aiken who listened to his calls with defense counsel, and then by the district court itself which denied Brandon representation during the suppression review.

After the district court ruled that Ranger Collins and ADA Aiken illegally listened to Brandon's telephone calls with his defense counsel, the Hunt County District Attorney's Office recused itself on October 2, 2007, and special counsel from the Attorney General's office took over the prosecution. Indeed, suppressing the forty-six pages of handwritten notes and the underlying phone conversations would have been an empty exercise if Aiken or anyone in her office remained on the case. The Hunt County District Attorney conceded the move was required because "appointment of special prosecutors would alleviate the Sixth Amendment violation since the new prosecutors would not listen to the defendant's telephone calls with the defense team." As defense lawyer Kathy Ferguson once again had aptly noted: "You can't un-listen to the tapes. We can't pull out of their minds what they may have heard."

Of course, although the District Attorney's Office no longer was on the case, Ranger Collins – the man who first listened to the recorded conversations and headed the investigative team – remained in place. Moreover, Joel Gibson from Hunt County Sheriff's Office also had received copies of the telephone conversations. Although Gibson said he did not listen to them, he conceded that others in his office may have. Furthermore, it turns out that the government may have learned a critical point from the eavesdropping which perhaps later guided trial strategy to Brandon's prejudice.

The appellate court which reviewed Brandon's conviction expressly noted that among the calls the government listened to included one in which "the defense counsel's secretary and Brandon discuss how [Michael] Etherington lied in his statement to the police." Incredibly, the appellate court then concluded that its review of this and the other calls "failed to discover any privileged information of even the most marginal value to the State," and "although not for lack of trying, the Hunt County District Attorney's Office failed to discover anything of value when it violated Brandon's constitutional rights." Not so.

The defense strategy to expose Mike Etherington's alleged lies would be of immense value to the prosecution team. Etherington was a key source for Ranger Collins in his supporting affidavit to obtain the arrest warrant, and a credibility assault against such a principal witness could have a devastating impact on the prosecution's case. However, the state decided not to call Mike Etherington as a government witness at trial, and query whether that calculation was made in part because it knew from the illegal eavesdropping that defense counsel would challenge him as an outright liar during cross-examination.

The unconstitutional intrusion into the attorney-client relationship was not the only dirty trick employed by the prosecution team against Brandon Woodruff. The new prosecutor, Adrienne McFarland, Assistant Texas Attorney General, had been with the AG's office since 1993, and she turned out to be every bit as shady as her predecessor Keli Aiken. In February 2009 on the eve of Brandon's trial the state prosecutors filed with the court a list of all the supposed bad things the teen boy had done over his entire life. In a criminal trial the prosecution can introduce evidence of other so-called bad acts by the defendant if they are relevant to the charged crime, e.g., the prior acts establish a similar pattern which sheds light on his modus operandi. However, such material often has a prejudicial impact against the defendant with a real risk that the jury may convict not based on the actual evidence for the charged crime but simply based on a general claim that the defendant is a bad person. Accordingly, the prosecution must establish that there is a logical nexus or transactional relationship between prior acts and the charged crime, and is prohibited from using this evidentiary tool as a cynical means for character assassination.

In Brandon's case, the state prosecutors stooped to a new low, and lacking meaningful evidence for the double murders, instead launched a smear campaign by filing a Notice of Intent to Introduce Extraneous Offenses. The prosecution was throwing the proverbial kitchen sink at Brandon Woodruff. In addition to including benign material such as skipping classes at school, running up minutes on his cell phone and maxing out his credit cards – describing half the teen population across the United States – the prosecution also identified the boy's homosexuality as an "extraneous offense," and stated "that on or about July and August 2005, in Dallas County, Texas, and Fort Lauderdale, Florida the defendant, Brandon Dale Woodruff, participated and/or starred in homosexual pornographic videos under the stage name 'Bradley Rivers.'"

There was no dispute that Brandon had done gay porn for Helix Studios. However, it had nothing to do with the murders, and certainly was not a bad act. Of course, a conservative jury packed with Christian fundamentalists from a small town in northeast Texas may not appreciate that gay porn is a legitimate pursuit under the First Amendment, and such jurors may develop a sinister opinion about the kind of boy who would do such a thing. Accordingly, at a pre-trial evidentiary hearing on February 16, 2009 the defense team moved to keep out any evidence about Brandon's involvement with gay porn, and Kathy Ferguson argued:

> There have been allegations that our client has participated in and starred in some pornographic videos of a gay nature, homosexual pornographic videos. And we just don't see how any of those are at all relevant to any theory of killing – committing the murder of his parents. And we think that is just there to inflame the passions of the jury knowing that Hunt County is very religious, very conservative county, that the effect of introducing those into evidence would be solely to turn the jury against Mr. Woodruff

and, again, paint him as a bad person. And any probative value that that might have is going to be grossly outweighed by the inflammatory and prejudicial nature of those films.

Ferguson further continued that the prosecution had not even provided her team with copies of the films: "they've provided us notice that they have copies of the videos, which we still as of today do not have, for us to review as the Defense team although we've been given copies of the CD case – or DVD case."

In response, assistant attorney general McFarland attempted to portray Brandon Woodruff as possibly involved with producing child pornography, and advised Judge Beacom that the prosecution did not afford the defense team with its right "to view these videos" because "some of the people that participated in the videos are potentially under the age of 18," and "it looks like they definitely could – it could include child pornography."

In fact, contrary to the loathsome representation from Adrienne McFarland, a so-called officer of the court, the performers definitely were not minors. Helix Studios was a major player in adult entertainment, and it played by the rules. Federal law requires production companies to maintain records concerning the age, identity and stage name of their actors. Indeed, Helix president Keith Miller provided in response to a subpoena all compliance material on Brandon Woodruff including a copy of his driver's license, and expressly invited the Texas investigators to contact him with any further needs.

The judge ruled against the prosecution, and would not allow it to introduce at trial any evidence that Brandon had performed in the gay flicks. And yet the prosecution still could declare victory in pushing its smear narrative against Brandon Woodruff. After all, in one slick move the state told the world that Brandon was gay and performed in porn, and further amplified its inflammatory impact by wrongly perpetuating the pernicious stereotype held by ignorant folks that there is a correlation between homosexuality and pedophilia. In June 2015 Attorney General Ken Paxton promoted Adrienne McFarland to become Deputy Attorney General, and she now is the Chief of all criminal investigations and prosecutions in the Lone Star State.

Although Brandon's involvement with gay porn was excluded from trial, the prosecution still had scored its point. The list of "extraneous offenses" was publicly filed on the court docket and covered by the local paper which disclosed all the salacious dirt to the small community from which the jury panel was assembled. Katherine Ferguson argued to the court that "this was put in the open records so that the newspapers and everyone else can get a hold of it," and "the State is trying to prejudice the potential jury pool in this county in the hopes that a jury will convict BRANDON DALE WOODRUFF of capital murder because he might be gay." At the February 16, 2009 hearing Ferguson further expressed her concern that this sharp practice would have a "prejudicial impact" on her client at the imminent trial:

> As the Court is aware, a week ago once their notice of extraneous offenses was filed, there was a big front page story splashed all over the paper about what the State may or may not try to prove. And we're concerned about prejudicial impact on Brandon, particularly, since at this point it looks as if we're about two weeks out from picking a jury.

The filed notice of "extraneous offenses" was replete with outright falsehoods, unsubstantiated rumors and irrelevant gossip.

Indeed, some of the outrageous claims had been fed to Ranger Collins in October 2005 by the subsequently discredited Mike Etherington, and accordingly, the state prosecutors knew or should have known they may be false in February 2009 when included in the Notice of Intent to Introduce Extraneous Offenses. For example, based on Etherington's gossip, the state prosecutors alleged "that on or about 2005, in Dallas and Taylor Counties, Texas, the defendant, Brandon Dale Woodruff, stripped and danced for money at La Bare and male strip and dance clubs in Dallas and Abilene." However, after speaking with the club's owner, Ranger Collins already had determined that Brandon never worked at LaBare, and at the gay clubs Brandon simply liked to dance with his shirt off which is common for the boys. The list of "extraneous offenses" also alleged "that on or about 2005, in Rockwall County, Texas, the defendant, Brandon Dale Woodruff, injected himself with steroids or consumed steroids." Once again, the investigators seemingly had rejected this allegation. Mike Etherington had told Ranger Collins that Brandon injected steroids which were supplied by Dustin Perry who worked at a veterinarian's hospital. However, Dustin denied that claim, and the porn videos in which Brandon performed reveals the rather unimpressive body of 19-year-old twink rather than a roid-pumped stud. Mike Etherington had a disturbing obsession with Brandon, and much of what he said about his one-time friend simply was wrong. The inclusion of this material in the filed notice of "extraneous offenses" by the state prosecutors in February 2009 was unconscionable given that

Ranger Collins already had written off Mike Etherington following the bum information he had provided in October 2005 for the supporting affidavit upon which the arrest warrant was based.

Sadly, the Texas Rangers and state prosecutors demonstrated time and again that neither Brandon's rights nor the truth much mattered.

8 MURDER WEAPONS?

Norma and Dennis Woodruff died from multiple stab wounds and gun shots to their faces and heads. At the time of Brandon's October 2005 arrest the knife and firearm had not been found which certainly posed a dilemma for law enforcement particularly since there was no other physical or direct evidence linking the boy to the gruesome crime. Two-and-a-half years later a knife was discovered under bizarre circumstances which the prosecution dubiously argued at trial was one of the murder weapons, and to this day the firearm still remains undiscovered although at trial the prosecution presented a fantastical theory tying Brandon to that supposed weapon.

On June 12, 2008 Brandon's sister Charla and aunts Kathy Lach and Linda Matthews were emptying out the metal barn at the Heath residence, and lo and behold a dagger wrapped in plastic was discovered in a box. Kathy said "I had read where his roommate said there was a dagger missing from his dorm room closet and the word 'dagger' stuck out," and "then when I saw that, it was a dagger, like a Gothic-looking dagger, and I just thought, oh, my goodness, this might be what they were looking for." The lab tested the dagger, and it had a single drop of Dennis Woodruff's blood under a decorative skull on the hilt. The state argued it finally had direct evidence to link Brandon Woodruff to his parents' murders. Indeed, as Ranger Collins stated in his interview with Investigation Discovery for the "Lone Star Mystery" episode in its *Nightmare Next Door* series, the discovery of the dagger was welcome news because the case still was largely circumstantial, and "a good piece of physical evidence would have bolstered the case tremendously."

Except not so fast. Lately-discovered evidence often can be suspiciously unreliable, and that was particularly so with the dagger. The Heath residence, barn and property were combed over on October 22, 2005 by eight law enforcement officers from multiple local, state and federal agencies, and no weapons were found. The search team even had deployed an ATF canine unit which "was trained in trying to locate a handgun or weapons." There simply was nothing discovered at the Heath premises. Indeed, specifically with respect to the barn, Hunt County detective Joel Gibson wrote in his report that "no evidence – no items of evidentiary value was located in the search of the barn." Moreover, family members previously had gone through the contents at the Heath property on multiple occasions, and never come upon this mysterious box with a dagger wrapped in plastic.

The excuse for not earlier finding the dagger was because the Heath barn was so packed investigators simply were overwhelmed in their search, and accordingly, actually did not look at everything. For example, Joel Gibson at trial walked back his original report that "no items of evidentiary value was located in the search of the barn," and instead explained "we attempted to search the barn but due to the amount of the contents that was in there and it was hard to be able to walk through the barn to be able to do a search." Further direct examination by the prosecution – in improper leading form, by the way – provides the following exchange with Detective Gibson:

> Q. So a decision was made to not go through every item that was in that barn.
>
> A. That's correct.
>
> Q. In fact, a decision was made to not go through every item or every box that was in that garage either.
>
> A. That's correct.

The new story hardly inspires confidence if it's to be believed at all. If Gibson is telling the truth, then shame on law enforcement that they did not bother to conduct an exhaustive search of the barn. After all, Randall Lunz saw Brandon Woodruff on the Heath driveway on Sunday evening, October 16 after the boy's earlier visit with his parents in Royse City, and by October 20 Ranger Collins had suspected Brandon Woodruff as their killer. So when the Heath premises were searched by an eight-man team plus a canine unit on October 22 it turns out the barn actually was not searched in a thorough fashion?

As a threshold matter, Brandon Woodruff denied ownership of the dagger found in the Heath barn, and said it was not the same one from his dorm room. Brandon apparently had gotten rid of his after roommate Eric Gentry's mother questioned whether ACU policy allowed it on campus. In speaking about Brandon's dagger Eric said the following:

> The first time I saw it was when he first moved in the dorm, he showed it to me. And my mother was

actually there when he showed it to me. And she said, you can't have this, Brandon. ACU has some rules about the length of the blade. You can carry a pocket knife if the blade is so long.

At trial the testimony from ACU classmates was unsure and inconsistent whether the dagger from the Heath barn was the same one they had seen in Brandon's dorm. The newly-discovered one was 18-inches long with a six-inch handle and a twelve-inch blade. However, Adrienne Linge testified that she did not remember the dagger she had seen in Brandon's room as being that long. Although Eric Gentry testified that the dagger introduced at trial was the same from the dorm room he originally told the Rangers – consistent with Adrienne's recollection – that Brandon's dagger only was six inches long.

The barn always was kept unlocked, and in the ensuing years after Brandon's arrest anybody could have acquired and planted a similar-style dagger. The dagger had only a single drop of blood from his father, and none from his mother. Given that the crime scene was a blood bath and the knife used was deeply plunged multiple times into the murdered couple, one would have expected more incriminating evidence from the dagger if it in fact were the murder weapon. A drop of well-placed blood certainly could be added to a planted dagger. The investigation team cleared out of the Heath premises within a week, and among the items left behind to which others had access was the bloody couch.

It just does not make sense that law enforcement would have missed the dagger in its search, and it's suspicious that it was discovered as trial approached. Upon Brandon's arrest Ranger Collins conceded "we're not saying at this point we got proof beyond a reasonable doubt at all," and he admitted that "a good piece of physical evidence would have bolstered the case tremendously." If Brandon were the killer and used that dagger, why would he just wipe and store it in the family barn which would be among the first places searched by law enforcement? To this day the firearm still has not been found, and it's simply illogical that Brandon would dispose the gun in one fashion and the dagger in another if he were responsible for his parents' murders. If Brandon were sophisticated enough to plan and clean-up his crime wouldn't he also understand that a blade could be matched to the wounds? It makes more sense that the dagger was a convenient plant against Brandon – albeit by whom is anybody's guess – rather than the murder weapon against his parents.

In fact, the medical examiner who did the pathology report on Dennis Woodruff – he suffered nine stab wounds whereas Norma had only one – could not conclude with any degree of scientific certainty that the discovered dagger was the murder weapon, and testified only that it was "possible" to the extent that "lots of knives are capable of causing those wounds" including "a kitchen knife." The defense argued that the ME's opinion about there even being a "possible" correlation between the dagger and the wounds was entitled to no weight given the failures to follow basic text-book procedures including measuring all the stab wounds and compressing them to determine whether they were consistent with a blunt- or sharp-edged blade. And heck, the medical examiner had not even seen the dagger from the barn until the day of trial – "today is the first time I've seen that knife" – and she never even took any measurements to determine the length, thickness or width of its blade.

Forensic pathologist Dr. Joy Carter, the former chief medical examiner for Washington, D.C., testified as the defense expert, and she emphatically concluded the dagger found in the barn and introduced at trial "is not the weapon that inflicted these wounds" because although "it's possible in some of these wounds" with respect to others "I would say that is completely inconsistent." For example, the dagger had two sharp edges but the wounds were caused by a knife with one blunt edge and one sharp edge, and Dr. Carter even concluded two knives were used because some of the wounds were rectangular. Although the appellate court ultimately affirmed Brandon's conviction, it only did so with great reluctance and expressly noted that "Dr. Carter's testimony is strong evidence contrary to the jury's verdict." The investigators thought the newly-discovered dagger in the Heath barn was like a gift under the Christmas tree but there's an old saying: if it seems too good to be true, it probably is.

The investigators never recovered the firearm which was used in murdering Brandon's parents. However, several large-caliber bullets were recovered at the scene, and a replica long-barreled Colt .45 was missing from the Lee household. The Colt .45 was used by the U.S. Cavalry during the Civil War and Indian Wars, and the powerful six-shooter could blast away man or beast. The state theorized that Brandon stole the iconic revolver while he was visiting Morgan at the Lee home on Saturday, and turned it against his parents on Sunday. Relying upon the claims of a jailhouse snitch the state believed that Brandon then tossed the firearm into Lake Hubbard en route from the crime scene in Royse City to the Heath home.

Firearms are ubiquitous throughout Texas, and the

state has no restrictions on ownership beyond the federal requirements. They're owned by cowboys and ranchers, sportsmen and collectors, and good folks exercising their self-defense rights under the Second Amendment, and all can be openly carried. In Texas many children grow up around firearms, and learn to handle them at an early age.

Brandon's barrel racing girlfriend Morgan Lee was a crack shot who had taken hunter safety courses, and her father Mike owned numerous firearms. However, Brandon never had much interest in guns. In high school Brandon bought a 12-gauge shotgun to once go skeet shooting with Morgan. He complained about the butt hurting his shoulder on the kickback, and then after just a few shots the gun jammed. Brandon traded it with Morgan's dad for a floor-lamp made from an old rifle, and said shooting "was just not his thing to do." Morgan's mother Miss Lee told Ranger Collins it was obvious that "Brandon was not comfortable around guns and did not really know how to use guns." Similarly, Mike Lee in an interview with Ranger Collins said "that Brandon did not seem to have a very good knowledge of guns, and did not seem like the type to commit such a crime." Eric Gentry knew Morgan through Brandon, and had arranged a guys-only deer hunting outing for New Year's Day 2005 on some property owned by Morgan's friend. Eric said "Brandon was supposed to go hunting with us" but when the day arrived he instead "ended up riding horses with Morgan."

The truth is that Brandon actually was a bit afraid of firearms. A shit kicker allegedly once pointed a relatively-harmless pellet gun at Brandon – characterized by the state prosecutors as a "high school prank" – which sent him running behind another for protection. Perhaps Brandon was gun shy due to his sister Charla's suicide attempt with their father's handgun in 2000 when just a 13-year-old boy. That event had traumatized the entire Woodruff family. Unlike Charla, Brandon never had "a fascination with guns."

Mike Lee was an avid hunter. Most of Mike's rifles and shotguns were kept in a locked safe at his office. However, for home protection he kept one long gun in a closet and a pistol in a nightstand. The replica Colt hung on display in a leather holster and bandolier from a bookcase in the open foyer-like space on the second floor at the top of the stairs. The large space was used as an exercise room which had a treadmill, weight station, elliptical bicycle and other fitness equipment. A bay window in this exercise room overlooked the backyard, and on either side of that window were bookcases. Miss Lee said the bookcases "went from floor level up to the ceiling, and they had books in them and trophies, antiques, cowboy stuff, like old stuff." The Colt .45 hung at eyelevel from the top corner of one bookcase, and Miss Lee essentially described it as a movie prop:

> The gun was one that my husband had gotten and it had wooden handles, it was old. It looked like a gun that was used – or seen in a movie like Tombstone, like one of those. And then there was leather tooled belt, loops on it that had bullets in the loops and up on the shelf – I just had it draped over the edge and some other old cowboy relic things up there.

The replica Colt was "old, heavy and big, with wood grips and a gold trigger," and its steel barrel had a bluing finish.

After news was released that Brandon's parents were dead Morgan's mother Michelle Lee advised law enforcement that the Colt .45 and several rounds from the ammo belt had been stolen. According to Ranger Collins on October 20

Miss Lee "provided the Hunt County Sheriff's Office with the leather gun belt that said weapon had been in and the leather belt had two (2) rounds of ammunition for the Long Colt in the belt."   Ranger Collins "observed that the ammunition provided by Michelle Lee is consistent with the projectiles retrieved from the bodies of Dennis and Norma Woodruff as well as the crime scene."   The investigators theorized that Brandon stole the firearm when he was in the Lee house on Saturday, and then used it against his parents on Sunday.   However, this speculative theory did not hold water any better than a bullet hole-ridden bucket.

As a threshold matter, no one knew when the Colt .45 actually went missing. In addition to the exercise room at the top of the stairs the second floor also had Morgan's bedroom on the right side and a TV room on the left. The master bedroom for Michelle and Mike Lee was on the first floor, and they rarely went upstairs. Miss Lee advised Ranger Collins that she "didn't really pay that much attention to that gun upstairs," and "it could have been gone for a while" and she "wouldn't have noticed it." Indeed, she said "that no one in the house knew for sure how long the gun had been missing."

The firearm was discovered missing in October 2005 only by happenstance. On Monday, October 17, Mike Lee was preparing for a Colorado deer hunting trip, and he went upstairs to grab a hat from the bookcase where he noticed that the Colt .45 was gone from the holster with several rounds of ammo ripped from the belt loops. Ranger Collins interviewed Michelle Lee on October 24, and his investigative report provided the following:

> Michelle LEE claimed that her (Michelle LEE's) husband, Michael LEE, was the first to notice the gun

> was missing and stated that he (Michael LEE) asked her (Michelle LEE) about the missing gun and also asked their (Michael and Michelle LEE's) youngest daughter Morgan LEE about the missing gun. Michelle LEE advised that Michael LEE noticed the gun missing on Monday morning, 10-17-05.

Mike Lee was interviewed on November 29, 2005, and he provided a nearly identical account:

> Mike stated he was getting his things together to leave on a hunting trip and noticed the gun was missing. Mike stated he did not know how long the gun had been missing but noticed it on October 17, 2005. Mike stated he asked his wife Michelle and his daughter Morgan if they knew what happened to the gun. Mike stated neither his wife nor his daughter knew the gun was missing.

The firearm could have been missing for months.

For example, on Friday, September 24, 2005, Morgan Lee threw a slumber party at the Rockwall house on Creekside Drive against her parents' permission while they were away in Poetry, TX overseeing construction of the new home. The naughty girl's overnight guests included Brandon's old shit-kicker friends Mike Etherington, Dustin Perry, Joe Hagaman and Gerardo "Gerry" Hinojosa. These boys all had been targets of Brandon's angry post on his MySpace page. At this point Hinojosa now was a Hunt County Reserve Deputy, and actually accompanied Miss Lee to the Sheriff's Office on October 20 when she brought over the holster and belt.

The slumber party occurred on the second floor of the Lee house where the movie room and Morgan's bedroom were located, and the guests would have seen the Colt .45 on display in passing multiple times through the trophy room in going from one room to another. However, none of them recalled seeing it. For example, Mike Etherington recounted for Ranger Collins a detailed layout of the second floor including where furniture was placed, and had excellent recall about the night's events such as who slept where – Mike slept in Morgan's bed in her room and the girl slept on one of the couches in the movie room. However, when asked if he saw the Colt .45, Mike haltingly answered: "No. I'm just watching my steps now. No, my memory as of now, no. If I don't remember for sure I'm going to say no." Unlike Brandon, Mike Etherington was comfortable around firearms, and told Ranger Collins he had some in his bedroom: "in my room I have a single shot .22, I have a 10-clip automatic .22 rifle and then in my closet I have a Winchester .270 deer rifle and that's a single shot," and "then my brother has in his gun closet we have his shotgun." Dustin Perry also told Ranger Collins that he never saw the Colt .45 on the night of the slumber party, and no word on whether he slept in the movie room with Morgan or Morgan's bedroom with Mike.

So only God and the thief really know how long the Colt .45 was missing. The Lees regularly kept the house unlocked – a fact known by the shit kickers according to Morgan – and a few years earlier another firearm had been stolen out of Mike Lee's truck. The idea that Brandon Woodruff stole the Colt .45 seems preposterous given his aversion to firearms. Indeed, it would seem that Brandon would have just dismissed the Colt replica as a decorative prop. Morgan Lee said the Western-style six-shooter "doesn't look like a real working gun at all" but "looks more like decoration, and Brandon never asked about it." The investigators could have dusted the leather holster and bandolier for fingerprints but apparently the keystone cops would rather speculate about who ripped out the firearm and bullets rather than develop any hard evidence. Incidentally, an ATF gunpowder-sniffing dog was unable to detect that any firearms or ammo were ever present in any vehicles driven that weekend by Brandon, and no gunshot residue was detected on any of Brandon's clothing or personal items.

In a pathetic bid to tie the Colt .45 to Brandon Woodruff the state prosecutors trotted out a jailhouse snitch. William Pardun was a degenerate addict and habitual criminal who was incarcerated in the Hunt County Detention Center, and he claimed that Brandon asked him on two occasions "how long a gun would stay submerged with wooden handles." The testimony inherently was incredible. Brandon Woodruff may be no rocket scientist but surely he understood that a steel gun – even with wooden grips – would not float, and indeed, if the boy in fact had taken the Colt .45 he'd certainly appreciate just how damn big and heavy the long-barreled six-shooter really is.

When prosecutors use a jailhouse snitch they're just throwing a Hail Mary. Pardun had a rap sheet going back thirty-five years which included four felony convictions. Moreover, Pardun conceded he was angry at Brandon whom he believed "kited me up" and gotten removed from the "medical tank." After the 2009 trial at which Pardon testified he continued his downward spiral, and repeatedly was convicted for driving under the influence of narcotics and alcohol. In 2014 the degenerate was arrested again for DWI, and this time the state threw the book at him. Upon his conviction William Pardun was given a seventy-five year prison term, and in 2016 the appellate court affirmed the strict sentence based on his incorrigible recidivism. In short, the testimony from Pardun that Brandon supposedly asked about a floating gun is best disregarded.

Of course, regardless of who stole the replica Colt, there still was no evidence that it even was the murder weapon. Heck, the firearm could have been stolen by someone simply because it was a cool piece – the same reason it was acquired by Mike Lee – rather than for any evil use. Simply because large-caliber projectiles were discovered at the scene hardly means that they were fired from Mike Lee's stolen Colt .45.

Indeed, the ballistics expert for the state prosecutors was unable to determine whether the recovered bullets were .44 or .45 caliber, and throughout Texas there are countless firearms which use such large-caliber ammo. Although the state's expert testified that the bullets were cast lead and hand loaded – so-called "cowboy loads" – he also testified that even these are relatively common: "hand-loading is a hobby of many people around the United States and around the world that allows someone to reload their own ammunition as opposed to buying it from the store," and "there are cast lead bullets that you can purchase from manufacturers." However, there was no evidence at trial that Mike Lee ever used such hand loaded bullets for his Colt .45.

The state's expert also testified that the bullets were fired from a gun with six lands and a right twist configuration – the configuration initiates the spin on the bullet through the barrel to ensure its stability or accuracy in flying to the target – and only two manufacturers, Yeager and Ruger, use this rifling configuration. However, there was no evidence on who made Mike Lee's replica Colt.

Accordingly, there was no evidence that the recovered

bullets were even of the same kind used for Mike Lee's missing gun. Of course, even if the same kind, the only way to determine if the bullets actually were fired from his gun would be to compare their unique identifying marks against it which was an impossible task since the replica Colt never was found.

The real kicker is there was no compelling evidence that Mike Lee's replica Colt was even an operational firearm at the time it was stolen. The cartridges in the belt loops literally had turned green from corrosion they were so old, and Mike Lee told Ranger Collins on October 24, 2005 that "the gun was more for decoration than anything else," and "the last time the pistol was fired was three (3) or four (4) years earlier." However, inexplicably Mike Lee did not testify at the March 2009 trial notwithstanding that he was the firearm owner, the one who discovered it missing and perhaps the only person with first-hand knowledge that it was functional at one time.

Instead, Mike's wife Miss Lee testified concerning the firearm, and her lack of knowledge about it became apparent when she testified she did not even know whether it was kept loaded. The prosecutor then asked her "do you know, had your husband ever fired that gun" before 2005, and Miss Lee answered "I would say within the year before." However, Mike Lee actually had told Ranger Collins during his October 2005 interview that it was at least three if not four years earlier when he last fired it. More fundamentally, there was no indication that Miss Lee had personal knowledge that her husband previously fired the Colt .45 – i.e., directly witnessing the event – rather than simply hearing about it from him which would have been inadmissible hearsay. In short, very likely there was absolutely no proper evidence at trial that the firearm was even a functional weapon.

To argue that the dagger found in the Heath barn and the firearm missing from the Lee home were weapons used by Brandon Woodruff to murder his parents is a bridge too far. The dagger was discovered two and a half years after the unsecured barn was first searched by law enforcement which likely makes it a plant, and there was no compelling evidence that its blade inflicted the wounds. No one knew how long the Colt .45 had been missing but Brandon's discomfort with firearms likely clears him as the thief, and there was no compelling evidence that the recovered bullets were even fired from it. How can Brandon Woodruff be convicted for killing his parents beyond a reasonable doubt when there's insufficient evidence that the newly-found dagger and the missing Colt replica were even the murder weapons?

9 HOMOPHOBIC TRIAL

A homophobic narrative against Brandon Woodruff ran from jury selection through closing argument.

The trial commenced with opening arguments on March 5, 2009, and jury selection was the day before. Texas assistant attorney generals McFarland and Ralph Guerrero, a 2003 graduate from Yale Law School, introduced themselves to the 100-member jury pool as heterosexual family-friendly folk with local ties. McFarland said "my dad's side of the family is from Wills Point so I used to come up to this neck of the woods a lot when I was a little girl," and dropped that "I've got two kids, 9 and 13, and they both survived the TAAS test yesterday, so my husband reports." And then in mentioning her junior colleague McFarland said "this is Ralph Guerraro," and "he's looking for the right girl, so – so, anyway, that's all I'm going to say."

The negative media about Brandon Woodruff in the local paper resulting from prosecution filings with false information had left an unmistakable impact on many within the jury pool. Unfortunately, Brad Kellar for the *Rockwall County Herald-Banner* largely just regurgitated prosecution documents rather than engaging in any critical challenge. The only photograph of Brandon used to accompany his coverage of the case was the unflattering mugshot of the boy in an orange jumpsuit. Many prospective jurors fully admitted they assumed from the local rag that Brandon was guilty. One said "I believe he killed his parents" because "we read that *Herald-Banner* seven days a week, and there are a lot of things that may not be right, but I don't think there's as many reports that I've heard on this that they could all be wrong." Similar opinions were pervasive throughout the jury pool. One said "from what I read in the media I felt like he was guilty," and another said "I have heard about the case and read about it, and I think he's guilty." Although many said they could put aside their preconceived opinions aside to fairly weigh the evidence at trial, how does one unring the bell once it's been rung? As one prospective juror stated: "from what I read in the paper at the time, at the time when I read all of that, I was led to believe from what I'd read that he's guilty," and "that is a seed that is in my mind."

The pool from which the jurors for trial were selected was conservative by any metric including views on the death penalty. The state earlier had waived the death penalty against Brandon Woodruff, and if convicted he automatically would receive life imprisonment without parole. The rationale for the state's unusual move was to spare the family any further suffering with Brandon's execution in the event of a guilty verdict since it already had suffered through the losses of Norma and Dennis. However, when the jury pool was advised that the death penalty was off the table, several of the more blood-thirsty citizens stated they could not serve. For example, one prospective juror said "it seems like the State has already tied the hands of the jury" and "decided what the outcome is going to be," and if "all we have to do is decide guilt or innocence" then "I'm going to have a hard time taking an oath for that." Many came right out with their unwillingness at the outset to spare Brandon. One ignoramus said "he must be guilty to be here," and knowing that she "could not live" with herself if unable to sentence him to death. It was a common sentiment. One prospective juror said "if the evidence is there and he's guilty," then an "eye for an eye." Similarly, another said "I don't believe if he's guilty beyond a doubt that we should have to feed someone the rest of his life, to take care of him you know." As one summed up his position: "I couldn't take an oath that says he won't get fried." Usually the prosecution is in the position of striking jurors who are unwilling to consider the death penalty; in Hunt County the prosecution had to strike jurors who were unable to accept a life term.

The jury pool was comprised largely of Christian evangelicals, and the hostility against homosexuality was open and unapologetic. One individual said "I wouldn't have a high opinion" of gay people, and "I would pray for them." Another said "I just have a less opinion of them" which "possibly" would make him "more likely to think that they're not truthful." Indeed, out of the twelve jurors and two alternates selected eight of them "feel or believe that being homosexual or gay is morally wrong" according to the voir dire during the selection process. Sure, the chosen ones all gratuitously represented that a defendant's homosexuality would not weigh into their decision on guilt or innocence. But would it be okay to impanel eight avowed white supremacists or Nazi sympathizers in a criminal trial involving a black or Jewish defendant? And yet eight Texans who by their own admission viewed homosexuals as morally inferior to heterosexuals were allowed onto the jury panel to judge a gay boy.

As a general matter "evidence of a defendant's homosexuality is not admissible if the defendant's sexual orientation is not an issue" due to its prejudicial effect, and "courts reviewing the admission of prejudicial evidence of a defendant's homosexuality . . . should weigh heavily the prevalence of anti-gay biases among judges and juries in determining whether to declare a mistrial or reverse a conviction" according to the legal treatise *Sexual Orientation and the Law* by the Harvard Law Review Association. For example, the widely-cited 1996 decision *State v. Ford*, 926 P.2d 245, from the Montana Supreme Court expressly recognized that "there will be, on virtually every jury, people who would find the lifestyle and sexual preferences of a homosexual or bisexual person offensive," and accordingly, "our criminal justice system must take the necessary precautions to assure that people are convicted based on evidence of guilt, and not on the basis of some inflammatory personal trait."

The state insisted that Brandon's homosexuality was "an issue" because it underpinned his supposed motivation for his parents' murders, and prosecutors repeatedly pounded to the jury during the 12-day trial that the young defendant was living a double life based on lies in which he ditched classes at ACU for gay adventures in wild Dallas. Faced with flunking out and returning home to a hick town the prosecutors argued that Brandon killed his disappointed parents for their life insurance – and a fancy truck – so he would be free to pursue his gay life with carefree abandon. "He's cashing in" state prosecutors argued before the jury, and "he's killed his parents and he is starting a new life." However, this theory was absurd on its face, and collapsed under its own weight. The prosecution essentially created this theory out of whole cloth with no underlying evidence in order to use it as a bootstrap argument for the introduction of the prejudicial fact that Brandon was gay.

As a threshold matter, Brandon was not even aware that his parents had life insurance in which he was a named beneficiary until after their deaths. Indeed, the family was financially stretched, and had accumulated substantial debt. Accordingly, the theory that Brandon was motivated to kill his parents for an economic windfall simply was not supported by any evidence. Moreover, Brandon sometimes had permission to use his mother's Silverado for various reasons – including when his own truck had issues – and other times had no problem taking it without permission. Although Brandon was flunking out of college and maxing out his credit cards – how many kids does that describe? – Brandon simply did not require financial support from his parents to embrace a new life in gay Dallas and avoid returning home. The cute twink was making easy cash in adult films, and had found an appreciative crowd in the big city. If Brandon Woodruff were as money-obsessed as the state prosecutors insisted then that hot number easily could have found a sugar daddy who'd put him up on short notice.

In fact, the robbery theory now advanced by state prosecutors was fundamentally inconsistent with the earlier conclusion by Ranger Collins and other investigators that personal rage was the killer's motivation. Norma and Dennis Woodruff were killed at close range involving multiple gunshot and stab wounds to their heads and faces. Although the prosecutors now were arguing at the 2009 trial that Brandon was motivated by self-gain, the lawmen who investigated the 2005 murders stuck to their guns in believing that the motivation involved a personal cause. The gruesome overkill certainly was not about Brandon taking a joy ride in a fancy truck or getting some payday to be gay as argued at trial by the state prosecutors. So what was the point of the repeated post-mortem stab wounds? There was no evidence that Brandon had any reason to hate his parents and – unlike his sister Charla – never had raged against them in the past.

The prosecution did not even believe its own bullshit theory that Brandon Woodruff was looking for a cash windfall to live a gay life by killing his parents, and in a candid moment before the jury panel admitted that it may never come out why the boy would have any reason to murder them:

> Why he did this? Is that something that we have to prove to you? And that may come out and it may not and you may eventually have different theories about what the motive could be, but it's not something that we have to prove beyond a reasonable doubt. It's not something that the 12 of you have to agree on. Okay?

This concession from the prosecution was a nod to the obvious: it simply did not make any sense for Brandon Woodruff to have murdered his parents. Of course, as Judge Judy often quips, if something doesn't make sense, it usually isn't true. However, the prosecution still had to cobble together some lame story on which the jury could hang its proverbial hat. Indeed, as one member from the pool stated: "if you don't have no reason to kill that person, what was the reason?" As a practical matter no one would vote to convict Brandon Woodruff in the absence of some narrative due to the flimsy evidence against him. The government only had circumstantial evidence – rather attenuated at that – against

Brandon Woodruff, and the question begged is why would the 19-year-old kill his parents? This was a Herculean task for the state prosecutors to answer given that Brandon and his folks by all accounts had a loving relationship, and his arrest was a complete shock to the community.

Judge Beacom – falsely advised earlier that the skin flicks in which Brandon appeared may be child porn – enjoyed a few snickers as the state introduced evidence about Brandon's homosexuality. The defense team had sought to keep out flirtatious texts from boyfriend Alex Rulli including one calling Brandon "sexy," another saying "I miss you," and one asking him to "come warm me up." In ruling that the text messages were not prejudicial to Brandon because they do not reflect homosexuality the judge quipped "I'm sure I've called another man sexy at some time in my life." Did Judge Beacom also tell another man in the same breath that "I miss you" and ask him to "come warm me up?"

The judge also allowed into evidence that Station 4, the Dallas club at which Brandon and his friends went dancing on Sunday night, was a gay establishment, and the jurist disingenuously reasoned that it was not prejudicial because Brandon's attendance did not necessarily reveal his orientation:

> Well, where they were that evening is definitely relevant and I don't know, do you have to be gay to go into a gay bar? I don't think so. I think it's open to anybody that wants to go so I'm not going to keep [a witness] from testifying about where they went or the nature of the facility where they went.

The judge's reason was specious in many respects. It's called a gay club precisely because most people there will be gay. As Alex Rulli testified, "a few" straight guys may visit Station 4 but otherwise going there was a "high indication" of being gay; after all, as Alex continued, the dance club was on the "gay strip down in Dallas and that's the main gay club." This presumption is so well understood by the general public that Robby Martinez told his girlfriend it was a straight club precisely because he did not want her getting any wrong ideas that he may be gay. Moreover, Judge Beacom never explained why it was "definitely relevant" that Station 4 was a gay place. Certainly Brandon's whereabouts were relevant during the alleged night of his parents' murders but the club's identity was completely irrelevant, and given the homophobic jury the prejudicial impact was outweighed by any evidentiary value. The jury simply could be told that Brandon Woodruff was at a dance club without saying it was full of dancing queens.

The state not only wrongly used Brandon's homosexuality as the purported motivation behind the double murders but further used the boy's tiered coming out process to undermine his credibility and paint him as sinister. Brandon steadfastly insisted that he did not kill his parents. However, in opening arguments the state told the jurors they should not believe Brandon "because he was a troubled young man who had been living too many lies for too long," and the central "lie" he supposedly perpetuated was his double life as a gay man.

This homophobic narrative apparently was planted to law enforcement by Brandon's sister Charla. After his arrest Charla visited Brandon at the Hunt County Detention Center on October 26 for no apparent purpose other than to cruelly badger him about being gay. During this jailhouse visit Charla repeatedly asked Brandon "are you gay," what was his relationship with Alex Rulli and whether Station 4 was a gay club.   Following that jailhouse visit Charla immediately marched over to see Ranger Collins, and little Miss Nancy Drew recounted the ambush she engineered against her brother:

> I said "Brandon, are you gay?" He said, "noooo." I said "are you gay?" And he said, "noooo." And I was like, "well, honey, there's this website that I looked at, and who is this firefighter? You're all having an awful good time. I want to make sure you had fun. Last weekend and another weekend." He said "that's my friend from Florida, he lives in Florida." I said, "okay there's a lot of guys on there Brandon, a lot of guys." He said, "I have a lot of gay friends." I said "well that's great, that's good for you."

Charla told Ranger Collins that Brandon "was living this whole other life," and further explained to the lawman that if Brandon could lie about the little things such as being gay, then as a marked liar he would have no credibility on big things such as committing murder:

> If you lie about little things but you're telling the truth about big things, they're going to know you're a liar, and they're not going to believe you. If you lie about these little bitty things then if you tell the truth about the big things they've already marked you as a liar and you're a liar to them and they don't care.

Ranger Collins swallowed hook, line and sinker, and in speaking about Brandon's so-called "alternative lifestyle" during subsequent interviews with other witnesses repeated the false tautology like a signature line that if you lie about the little things, then you will lie about the big things.

A "little thing"? A teenage boy coming to terms with

his sexual orientation is not a "little thing." If being gay were such a "little thing," then how come Brandon's church and college did not approve of homosexuality and marriage equality? Their Bible calls "homosexuality an abomination punishable by death." If such a "little thing," then why did Brandon's shit kicker friends make such derisive comments about queers? If such a "little thing," then why was Brandon's family so concerned? His father Dennis called it a "dangerous lifestyle" and his sister Charla allegedly called him a "fucking faggot." If such a "little thing," then why in 2003 did Texas engage in a court fight to keep gay sex between consenting adults on the books as a criminal act? When Brandon Woodruff was just a little boy his church, family and state certainly did not treat homosexuality as a "little thing."

The state was relentless in mischaracterizing the ordinary coming out process by Brandon as reflecting a double life in order to paint him as a sinister soul. The state compared the "truth vs. fiction" about Brandon Woodruff as follows:

> Before the Summer of 2005, [Brandon] dressed like a cowboy; trained horses; and dated Morgan, his high school girlfriend. Starting that Summer, [Brandon] began dying his hair; wearing Armani clothes; claiming he was a model; and partying with and dating gay Dallas men. His Dallas friends did not know about his old Rockwall life and his family and high school friends did not know about his new gay lifestyle.

At trial the state prosecutors in opening argument expressly told the jury panel that "Brandon Woodruff stands charged with capital murder because his lies finally caught up with him." The state characterized Brandon's closeted years during high school as a "fiction" exposed by the "truth" of his subsequent coming out, and argued that this was evidence Brandon Woodruff had a duplicitous mind.

A gay boy is closeted growing up in his early years not because he intends to deceive the world to gain some benefit but simply because he's still in the process of discovering himself, and is not yet ready to navigate through a homophobic world. The state took issue that once in college Brandon had developed a "new gay lifestyle" in Dallas, and as a 19-year-old freshman had not yet shared that knowledge with his old friends. However, as Brandon said:

> I didn't think I needed to jump up and down with a rainbow flag and say "Hey, I might be gay." Because myself I was kind of just going through that initial phase where you don't know and you don't know who to tell and you don't know going on with you. And so did I keep that part private from some people? Yes. Did I not tell everybody fully what was going on in Brandon's mind on a sexual level? I did keep that from people but I didn't think it was anybody's business.

Exactly how soon should Brandon have disclosed his "new gay lifestyle" – as the prosecution called it – to the whole world in order not to be branded with a double life at a criminal trial? Brandon's coming out process was no different than it is for countless young gay men who often confide to family members and old friends only after first comfortably finding their own place in the gay world.

One thing is clear: Brandon Woodruff never lied to law enforcement about his sexual orientation. Indeed, as Brandon correctly characterizes his interview with Jeff Collins, "when the Ranger asked me where I went that night I told him I went to Station 4 which is a gay club." However, Brandon continued, "the Ranger never once asked me, he never once asked me if I were gay. He never once asked me was I experimenting or nothing or I would have been honest with him."

In closing argument defense lawyer Katherine Ferguson soundly rejected the prosecution thesis that if Brandon were lying about being gay, then he must be lying about not killing his parents:

> [T]he most offensive part of this prosecution is the fact that the State wants you to infer that because Brandon Woodruff is either gay or bi-sexual, he must be a murderer. If he's going to lie to people about his sexual identity, he's guilty of killing people. That is the most offensive part of this case. The prosecution is hoping, relying on the evil assumption that you will be, because we're small-town east Texas, that you're going to be blinded by prejudice and say, if he's gay or bi-sexual, well, then he must be a murderer. That's offensive. It offends me. And I hope it's offended you.

Incredibly, the state prosecutors in their closing argument took the homophobic narrative one step further. They argued that not only did Brandon's supposed lies about being gay mean he could lie about killing his parents but he was compelled to kill like The Talented Mr. Ripley once his double lives – "fiction versus truth" – collided with each other as creeping "reality" encroached upon his "fantasy world":

> Knowing that he was going to murder his parents helps explain why he chose that Sunday to tell his dad that he is gay. He knew that his parents would not be

around to disapprove or otherwise interfere with his life. Maybe he felt that with them dead he would not have to hide his gay lifestyle any more.

In closing argument before a straight jury which believed in the moral inferiority of the gay lifestyle, Texas assistant attorney general Adrienne McFarland fully laid out her homophobic ugliness against Brandon Woodruff:

> Turning your attention to the weekend of the 15th and the 16th of October. His two worlds were colliding. He had been living these two separate lives. The one life where he's in 4-H and he's Morgan's boyfriend and he's an ACU student. And the other life where he's out partying with his friends in Dallas. He has a boyfriend. They know nothing about his other life.

> And that weekend is so important as it's leading up to what happened on Sunday night, because you look at what he did from the time he got in town on Friday night when he's dropped off — when he drops off Robert Martinez at Janssen Herring's apartment, what does he say, well, I'm in a hurry, I've got a party to go to. So he goes to a party in Dallas probably.

> By early the next morning, he's at Morgan's house, okay, switch back over to the other life. Goes with her that day, brings her Sonic in the morning and brings her gifts. They go get the lamb. Go out that night. And then what does he do? As soon as he drops her off, he's heading back to Dallas. You saw the toll records. He's partying with his friends in Dallas again Saturday night after he drops his girlfriend off.

Next morning switches back over to the other life. Now he's with his family and he's helping them out and he's doing stuff. And he's with Morgan some that day at the Ag barn. And then, finally, what happens, he goes back to Dallas again. Partying in Dallas again. But the thing that's interesting about this, is that on the 16th, he allowed these worlds to collide because he didn't care anymore.

He knew that his life as an ACU student was over. He wanted to tell his parents he was gay that weekend. This was all part of the plan. He wanted to confront them and tell them. And he goes to S4 with a friend from college, Robert Martinez. His Dallas friends said we've never met anybody before from his other world, from high school or from ACU.

He doesn't care anymore at that point because he knows that life is over. He's cashing in, he's killed his parents, and he's starting a new life. He's going to get those insurance proceeds and he's moving on. So he doesn't care what his friends at ACU think anymore. It's okay for those worlds to come together.

There simply was no evidence that Brandon Woodruff was compelled to kill his parents in order to live openly as a gay man. The cockamamie theory posited by state prosecutors that Brandon Woodruff was so conflicted that he felt only by getting rid of his unsupportive parents could he liberate himself from closet hell not only is a homophobic narrative but not supported by the factual record.

As discussed earlier, economic self-gain could not have been a motivating factor because Brandon knew his parents were financially strapped and was not aware of the life insurance until after their deaths. Moreover, Brandon's "two worlds" were not colliding as misleadingly portrayed by the state prosecutors. Indeed, Brandon was not nearly as closeted as the prosecution insisted. Many of Brandon's boyhood friends in Rockwall and even some of his new ones at ACU suspected he was gay even if he had not expressly disclosed it to them. Brandon never officially "came out" to the "shit kickers" because he did not like their ignorant attitudes and no longer ran with them. Brandon expressly told Ranger Collins in October 2015 he had started a new life, and was done with the good ole boys: "I'm through with Rockwall. I was doing my own thing. You know what I'm saying?"

And other than Eric Gentry, Brandon had known his new friends at ACU for only a few weeks, and given the school's position on homosexuality revealing his sexual orientation just would have resulted in needless drama. Given that Brandon had been dropped from several classes for repeated absences and would not be returning to ACU for the next semester what would be the point in telling his classmates about being gay? Brandon Woodruff was on a steady path of embracing his gay identity since spring 2005, and for all practical purposes – as reflected by the gay content on his MySpace page for all to see – that was the only world in which he was living by fall 2005.

In any event, there was nothing duplicitous about the coming out process for Brandon Woodruff; it was an ordinary journey for a gay teen who was born into a world which presumed he would grow up to be straight. Brandon Woodruff had found gay friends he liked, was dating, and exploring a more adventuresome side through porn work all without apology, and no one testified that he had any self-loathing or internalized struggles about being gay.

Brandon had an independent streak, and he certainly did not need his parents' blessing in order to be openly gay. Heck, Brandon was hitting the gay clubs in Dallas since his senior year in high school, and one press account reported that his mother Norma had confided to a family friend that she had become "exasperated" that "her son had become increasingly defiant in his late teens." Brandon hardly sounds like a momma's boy at her apron strings, and no doubt he was going to live his life the way he wanted regardless of whether it disappointed his family's Christian beliefs. Indeed, Norma and Dennis Woodruff had known for several months that Brandon likely was gay, and the state prosecutors simply were wrong in telling the jury that he first told them on Sunday afternoon, October 16. Although Dennis Woodruff that day told his sister Kathy Lach for the first time Brandon was gay, father and son previously had discussed the issue.

More fundamentally, Norma and Dennis Woodruff simply were not intolerant people who damned others to hell over their sexuality even if they held reservations about their teenage son coming out as gay. There's a big difference between hateful bigots and concerned parents, and Brandon's folks were in the latter camp. After all, there are real dangers for queer kids in a hostile world. However, Brandon's parents were not rejecting or "shunning" their son over being gay. Brandon said it best about his relationship with them: "I loved my parents and whether straight, gay, or confused, my parents loved me unconditionally. Nothing could stop my parents from loving me." Whatever issues or difficulties they faced or confronted the Woodruff family would work through them. One thing is for damn sure: Brandon

Woodruff was not motivated to kill his parents either to collect a payday or to live openly as gay, and there simply is no evidence to support that cockamamie theory advanced by the prosecution.

The trial record tangibly demonstrates that the homophobic "double life" argument was a successful tactic in turning minds against Brandon Woodruff. For example, Robert Martinez still presumed Brandon Woodruff was straight even after their trip to Station 4 on Sunday evening, October 16. The college athlete was interviewed by investigators on November 2. At the outset Ranger Collins said to him "I know with ACU being a Christian college and all that you may be uncomfortable about where you were in the early morning hours but we need to know that information." Robby quickly blurted back "I'm not gay, and I want to get that out." In speaking about Brandon's homosexuality the Ranger then said "if somebody will lie about something little like they'll lie about something big obviously." Robert agreed by saying "I didn't know" that Brandon was gay, and learning that "changed my view about him a little bit."

The prejudicial effect similarly was evident when Eric Gentry learned that his boyhood friend and ACU roommate was gay. Eric originally told the Ranger that he did not believe Brandon was capable of murder. In November 2005 when interviewed the young Bible-studies major adamantly told Ranger Collins "the Brandon I know is incapable of doing it." Eric continued about Brandon:

> Couldn't do it. He's kind of a pansy. I just don't think there's a way he could have brought himself to do it. The nicest guy you'll ever meet. Was there some other Brandon? I don't know about it. And

I'm his best friend.

However, the investigators flipped his opinion by disclosing that Brandon liked guys. At trial state prosecutors asked Eric "would it be fair to say that the Brandon you thought you knew was not the Brandon you knew" to which he answered "yes." And then they immediately followed up with the question: "Is it fair to say that your opinion that you expressed to the Rangers back in November of 2005 as to his capability of doing this has changed?" An objection from defense counsel was sustained which precluded an answer but the question was left hanging before the jury which exposed the homophobic game state prosecutors were cynically playing. In order to bring down Brandon Woodruff the state smeared the queer.

10 JURY VERDICT

The jury convicted Brandon Woodruff on March 20, 2009 after only five hours of deliberation. The state earlier had waived the death penalty, and the young man automatically was sentenced to a life term behind bars without parole.

Immediately after the conviction his defense counsel Katherine Ferguson told gay paper *Dallas Voice* in a March 26, 2009 article that in prosecuting Brandon Woodruff the state deployed a "strategy to highlight his sexual orientation," and Ferguson had argued to the jury that prosecutors were equating "gay" with "murderer." Ferguson further told the *Dallas Voice*:

> "They certainly wanted to ram that point down the jury's throat every moment they could," Ferguson told *Dallas Voice* this week. "They were hoping that this would be a small-town East Texas jury, and they would be so blinded by that issue that they would not sit back and examine the facts of the case. My whole attitude was, I didn't really care who he slept with. My concern was, did he murder his parents? And could the state prove it beyond a reasonable doubt?

And I don't feel the state did, but obviously the jury
disagreed."
Ferguson's assessment that a homophobic narrative rather
than underlying evidence resulted in Brandon's conviction
cannot be easily dismissed.

Indeed, a three-judge panel from the Sixth District
Court of Appeals in Texarkana, TX expressly told state
prosecutors in reviewing Brandon's conviction that "there are
a lot of things that we are concerned with." Although the
court ultimately affirmed the jury verdict its 2010 decision
Woodruff v. State, 330 S.W.3d 709 expressly called out the
evidentiary issues concerning whether the newly-discovered
dagger in the family barn or the missing firearm from the Lee
household even were the murder weapons. However, the
appeals process is gamed in the state's favor, and the
appellate judges held that "in reviewing the evidence for
sufficiency, we consider the evidence in the light most
favorable to the verdict."

Brandon Woodruff then sought review of his
conviction in federal court. He filed a writ of habeas corpus,
Woodruff v. Davis, No. 3:15-CV-1832-M, in United States
District Court for the Northern District of Texas, challenging
the government eavesdropping on his telephone
conversations with defense counsel. However, District Judge
Barbara M.G. Lynn rejected the writ on January 30, 2018
because "the dismissal of an indictment is not an appropriate
remedy absent prejudice, even if the Sixth Amendment
violation was deliberate," and characterized the request for
the 46 pages of handwritten notes by ADA Keli Aiken on the
telephone calls as nothing more than a "fishing expedition."
More fully:

Petitioner does not explain how he was prejudiced in

light of the suppression of any evidence obtained from the recordings, the recusal of the DA's Office, the appointment of a special prosecutor, and the order barring communication between the special prosecutor and the DA's Office about the case. He does not allege or suggest that the special prosecutor and the DA's Office communicated about the case in violation of the court order.

However, the federal decision ignores critical points. Ranger Collins also listened to some conversations between Brandon Woodruff and the defense team, and yet he remained involved with the case under both the DA's Office and the Texas Attorney General's Office. Moreover, one of those monitored calls involved Brandon Woodruff telling his defense team that Mike Etherington lied in his statements to Ranger Collins, and then the state at trial failed to call him as a witness. Did the Attorney General's office decide against calling Mike Etherington because it knew from the earlier eavesdropping that defense lawyers had an effective basis on which to cross-examine him? It's certainly a curious coincidence if not circumstantial evidence of perhaps something more sinister.

There is little reason for public trust in Texas justice. The arrest warrant against Brandon Woodruff was secured with a faulty affidavit comprised largely of meaningless gossip if not outright lies. Blunders were pervasive throughout the investigation. The cell phone tower records which would have established Brandon's whereabouts were not obtained. Brandon's phone on which he was talking and texting supposedly while simultaneously committing his parents' murders was not even tested for their blood, and the leather holster and bandolier from which the Colt .45 and ammo were ripped did not get dusted for his fingerprints. The dagger was discovered in an unsecure barn thirty months after investigators already had searched it, and there was no evidence that the missing firearm was operational or the recovered bullets had been fired from it. Even the appellate court which reviewed Brandon's conviction had serious doubt about the so-called murder weapons. The District Attorney's Office violated the defendant's Sixth Amendment rights and then the Attorney General's Office engaged in a smear campaign against him. Brandon Woodruff did not even get an impartial jury, and eight members believed that homosexuals are morally inferior. In place of real evidence the prosecution used a cockamamie theory to convict Brandon Woodruff.

In short, Brandon Woodruff was railroaded, and the courts which were supposed to protect his rights instead bent over backward to protect the government's case. Insufficient evidence? The court reviewed it all in the light most favorable to the state. Constitutional violation? The court insisted upon prejudice. In theory, the U.S. Constitution is designed to protect criminal defendants but in practice is a meaningless framework. The constitutional guarantees are empty promises. What the founding fathers giveth, the legal system taketh away.

The courts may believe they have carefully-constructed legal justification to excuse every wrong against Brandon Woodruff; however, doesn't there come a point that the cumulative effect of all the aggregated wrongs – from the investigative blunders to the dirty tricks, from the insufficient evidence to the homophobic narrative – becomes so overwhelming that no public confidence can be placed in the resulting conviction? The prejudicial sum is greater than the wrongful parts. Any fair-minded person viscerally understands that Brandon Woodruff was denied a fair trial, and no amount of judicial sophistry pursuant to parsed caselaw can cover up this fundamental injustice.

Indeed, there's a real possibility that an innocent man is sitting behind bars for a life term without parole on a wrongful conviction. The ugly truth is that the so-called criminal justice system gets it wrong more often than the people care to admit. Samuel R. Gross, a law professor at the University of Michigan who edits the National Registry of Exonerations, says in a July 24, 2015 op-ed for *The Washington Post* that according to a 2014 study he co-authored "4.1 percent of defendants who are sentenced to death in the United States are later shown to be innocent." That's 1 in 25. "Death sentences are uniquely well-documented" Professor Gross writes but "we don't know nearly enough about other kinds of criminal cases to estimate the rate of wrongful convictions for those." However, "in a country with millions of criminal convictions a year and more than 2 million people behind bars even 1 percent amounts to tens of thousands of tragic errors."

Following his conviction Brandon Woodruff submitted to a polygraph examination which concluded the boy was truthful in denying that he killed his parents, and that result was independently corroborated by a subsequent test by another examiner. The statistical odds that two examinations both would erroneously indicate a truthful response are less than two percent. The polygraph results were submitted to the federal court in the habeas proceeding, and the legal memorandum filed by Brandon's attorney provides the following:

After Mr. Woodruff exhausted his appellate rights, Eric Holden, one of the most respected polygraph examiners in the nation, administered a polygraph examination on whether Mr. Woodruff murdered his parents. Mr. Woodruff denied that he killed his parents and the test indicated his response was truthful. To further corroborate this result a different polygrapher re-examined Mr. Woodruff on the same question and Mr. Woodruff again showed to be truthful. According to studies addressing the reliability of polygraph examinations the chances of two properly conducted polygraph examinations both erroneously showing a truthful response are less than two-percent.

In rejecting Brandon's federal challenge the district judge simply ignored the polygraph results which indicated his innocence.

Many family members, long-time friends and other supporters including an increasing contingent from the LGBT community steadfastly have remained by Brandon's side, and the polygraph results did not tell them anything they did not already know. The people who know Brandon best know that he did not murder his parents, and nothing about the case against him makes any sense. Among those who continue to believe in Brandon Woodruff are his grandmother Bonnie Woodruff, his onetime employer Ede Bullock from Chisholm Feed, and Beckie Wilson who was a close friend and co-worker of Dennis Woodruff.

Brandon breaks down in rolling sobs when speaking from prison about his grandmother in an interview with Scott Poggensee who is producing the documentary film *Texas Justice* about the case:

My grandmother is like my angel. I smile even bringing up her name. She is just one of the biggest supporters I can have. She's been behind me this whole time, and she's believed in me from day one. She's told me to never give up. She's my everything. My grandmother has always, always, always just been there for me, and she's always given me hope. She told me I believe you, and that means more to me than anything else because she knows the truth.

Brandon confides that "prison can be very depressing at times, even when you're guilty," and "imagine being locked up in prison when you're not guilty."

Inmates only can meet with their visitors through a glass partition, and Brandon has not had any physical contact with his family since his 2005 arrest. This is a dehumanizing condition, and in speaking about his g-maw Brandon says that "I just look forward to being able to get to hug her." Of course, he'll never hug his parents again, and Brandon thinks of them as "angels" who are "watching over me until something else happens." In addition to producing the documentary Scott Poggensee also has launched an online campaign at freebrandon.org to bring attention to the case, and Brandon Woodruff hopes to have the Texas Court of Criminal Appeals accept a discretionary appeal for a complete review of the numerous issues raised by his dubious conviction.

One person who never believed in Brandon was his sister Charla Woodruff, and she has had no contact with him since October 26, 2005 after visiting him at the Hunt County Detention Center where she badgered him about being gay. During her subsequent meeting that same day with Ranger Collins, Charla spoke about her jailed brother:

At this point I don't think he's mentally sound. Even if he was before he went in there he's definitely not now. Do I think he'll last a hundred years in there? No. He'll probably be gone out of there by the time he's like 50. He'll have a heart attack or mental breakdown or something. He wouldn't last very long. Indeed, Charla told Ranger Collins just days after Brandon was arrested that she did not even want him out on bail while awaiting trial. The final words from Brandon Woodruff to his sister during that jailhouse visit so long ago were: "I didn't do it, I didn't do it."

ABOUT THE AUTHOR

Phillip Crawford Jr. is a retired attorney from the New York bar. He attended Bates College in Lewiston, Maine from which he graduated with a B.A. in English in 1985. At Bates he was President of the Gay-Straight Alliance, and in 1983 spearheaded a campaign to oust military recruiters from the campus for their discriminatory policies against the LGBT community. He attended George Washington University Law School where he was a Notes Editor for the *Law Review*. After graduating with highest honors as class salutatorian in 1988 he clerked for Chief Judge Judith W. Rogers on the D.C. Court of Appeals, and then with Judge George H. Revercomb on the United States District Court for the District of Columbia. He practiced law for fifteen years in New York City including several years with the plaintiffs' class action bar, and then retired after exposing his concerns about billing practices. Professor Lester Brickman characterized him in *Lawyer Barons* as a "whistle blower." Crawford also is the author of *The Mafia and the Gays* about the historic role of organized crime in LGBT nightlife.